G. R. F. Ferrari
City and Soul in Plato's *Republic*

D1556530

Lecturae Platonis

Edited by Maurizio Migliori

G. R. F. Ferrari

City and Soul
in Plato's *Republic*

The University of Chicago Press
Chicago and London

The University of Chicago Press, Chicago 60637
Copyright © Academia Verlag
All rights reserved. Published by arrangement with Academia Verlag, Sankt Augustin
First published in 2003 with the support of the University of Macerata, Italy
University of Chicago Press edition 2005

Printed in the United States of America
18 17 16 15 14 13 12 11 10 09   2 3 4 5 6
ISBN-13: 978-0-226-24437-2 (paper)
ISBN-10: 0-226-24437-7 (paper)

Library of Congress Cataloging-in-Publication Data

Ferrari, G. R. F. (Giovanni R. F.)
   City and soul in Plato's Republic / G. R. F. Ferrari.
      p.   cm.
   "Lecturae Platonis March 1999, University of Macerata, Italy, Department of Philosophy
and Humanities."
   Originally published: Sankt Augustin : Academia Verlag, 2003.
   Includes bibliographical references and index.
   ISBN 0-226-24437-7 (pbk : alk. paper)
   1. Plato. Republic. 2. Political science—Philosophy. I. Title.

JC71 .P6F47 2005
321'.07—dc22

                                                                    2005043720

   ♾ The paper used in this publication meets the minimum requirements
       of the American National Standard for Information Sciences—
   Permanence of Paper for Printed Library Materials, ANSI z39.48-1992.

Contents

Preface

In this short book I attempt to say what Plato is getting at in the *Republic*. That is a grand ambition for a slim volume. My strategy has been to trace one bright thread, the comparison between the structure of a society and that of the individual soul, a theme that runs through the *Republic* and binds its argument. After some close-drawn critique in chapter two, where I fasten on current misunderstandings of the analogy between city and soul, the remaining chapters have a more open texture. I argue there for a quite different understanding of how Plato's comparison of city and soul works and of what its point is; I situate the comparison in the larger contexts of ancient rhetorical theory and of intellectual rivalry, above all the rivalry between Plato and Isocrates; and towards the end I give an account of the tyrant and the philosopher-king as a matched pair who in their different ways break with the terms of the city-soul analogy - a break which reveals the characters and motives of both. By that point I am applying what I have learned from the city-soul analogy to some very familiar themes in the interpretation of the *Republic* - the sincerity of its utopianism, the justice of the philosopher's return to the Cave. Any topic of real importance to the interpretation of the *Republic* belongs in a web of connections with any other; a single leading thread can touch on the pattern of the whole.

In lieu of an introduction I offer in the opening chapter a study of Glaucon and Adeimantus - of their characters, their desires, their reasons for challenging Socrates - in the course of which the argument of the remaining chapters comes into view. For the city-soul analogy is proposed by Socrates as a response to the brothers' challenge, and it turns out to respond to their deepest needs.

The book has its origin in a series of lectures delivered in Italian to the philosophy department of the University of Macerata in 1999, as that year's contribution to the *Lecturae Platonis*. In preparing an English version for publication I have discarded many of the ideas with which I happily experimented in those lectures; but I have tried to retain in writing the forthrightness of speech, if not its informality. The reader will not find many caveats in these pages, but must supply them for himself; and he will find no discursive footnotes at all. In their place I have attached to each chapter an acknowledgment of only the most direct influences on its themes and a brief account of the current interpretations that form its working context.

Kate Toll read an early draft of chapter one, Rachana Kamtekar an early draft of chapters two, three, and four; Hayden Ausland and Sara Rappe read a near-final draft of the entire book. I thank them all for their time and for their friendly and beneficial input, and I thank Sara in particular for her warm encouragement. I presented an early version of the book's main ideas to audiences at Pennsylvania State University and at Boston University, and garnered helpful written comments from Joseph Cotter at the first, and from Charles Griswold and David Roochnik at the second. The students in my graduate seminar on the *Republic* were an unfailing resource of sharp analysis tempered with good cheer, and the written comments of Agnes Gellen and of Suzanne Obdrzalek were especially helpful to me as I recast chapter one. My colleagues in the Classics department at Berkeley - I believe Mark Griffith's was the door I knocked on most often - were generous with their store of parallels from Greek literature and their bibliographic knowledge. I also made use of wise but anonymous comments on a very early draft of the book that was submitted to a committee of scholars who were kind enough to assess my work for a promotion case.

My greatest debt is of course to Maurizio Migliori and to his team of students and young colleagues at the University of Macerata, both for the invitation to give the original lectures and for the lively debate and exceptionally warm hospitality with which I was regaled during my stay. I thank Maurizio for the energy he has devoted to the *Lecturae Platonis* and for his forbearance as I rethought and rewrote my contribution to the series. In the pages of the Italian translation that is to follow (ed. Morcelliana), which will contain an appendix of comment and authorial response, I shall be delighted to renew our intellectual exchange.

CHAPTER 1

The Brothers

1. The house of Cephalus

We would not know of Plato's brothers Glaucon and Adeimantus were it not through their relationship to Plato. They did not make an independent mark on the historical record. Yet as scions of a prominent family, of aristocratic lineage on both sides, they were in a position to do so. In particular, they counted among their kinsmen two members of the Thirty, the oligarchic, pro-Spartan junta that Sparta imposed on Athens at the end of the Peloponnesian War, and that perpetrated a brief reign of terror under the leadership of one of those kinsmen, Critias, before democracy was restored. If the *Seventh Letter* is to be trusted, Plato was invited to join the oligarchic project. It held some attraction for him, he writes (324c-326b); but not for long. The junta that was to purge the city of unjust men and imbue it with virtue and justice - so ran the slogan - soon descended to atrocities. Plato kept his distance.

He is certainly at pains to lay the shadow of the Thirty and of its bloody failure over the *Republic*'s opening pages, most obviously by staging the discussion at the house of Cephalus. Both sons of this wealthy metic were to suffer under the Thirty, with Polemarchus murdered for his money and Lysias escaping into exile. It is striking, then, that Plato makes Glaucon and Adeimantus the best of friends with these young men whose prosperity and happiness close members of their family will later destroy.

When Adeimantus first appears, it is in the company of Polemarchus and of Niceratus, Nicias' son (327c). They are young friends out to have fun. Just returned from viewing the Bendis' Day parade together, they are looking forward to a celebratory barbecue at Cephalus' house, and excited about the all-night festival to follow. Later, in Book 5, we will see Polemarchus whisper together with Adeimantus, touching him by the cloak and pulling him close (449b). If Glaucon appears first in Socrates' company rather than theirs, he seems quite as much at home in Cephalus' house as his brother. When Glaucon shows up unexpectedly at Cephalus' door in the company of Socrates and the others, it is only Socrates whose presence draws Cephalus' attention, and only Socrates whom he chides for the infrequency of his visits (328d). Glaucon is part of the regular circle.

It is also a cultured circle. Already at the house is the rhetoric teacher Thrasymachus (328b). Cephalus expresses his regret at not having more opportunity for intellectual conversation with Socrates, and urges him to come more often and to think of his household as family (328d). Polemarchus, not confined to home like his aged father, is on bantering terms with Socrates (327c), and once the discussion is under way will burst in with a quotation from the poet Simonides (331d-e). Niceratus seems a good friend, and the concern that Nicias took over his son's intellectual development is something of a theme in Socratic literature, appearing both in Plato's *Laches* (200c-d) and Xenophon's *Symposium* (3.5). Above all, Cephalus' is a household in which the delights of an all-night festival can be passed over for the delights of an all-night discussion.

The metics at Athens were immigrants (μέτοικοι), resident aliens. They were disbarred from holding political office and so from becoming central figures in the public life of the city in which they chose, nevertheless, to make their home. If, like Cephalus, they tended to transfer their energies to money-making, this activity evidently did not entail a sacrifice of education and culture. Cephalus is very content to have been only a middling businessman by comparison with his grandfather (330b), and seems more concerned about his sons' education than about money (328d). His wealthy family moves in the very best circles at Athens.

But although Adeimantus and Glaucon treat Cephalus' sons as equals, this is not because disbarment from political office counted for little in their society. Further on in the *Republic* Socrates passes a comment on metics remarkable for its offhandedness, when you consider who is in his audience. Describing in Book 8 how a democracy degenerates into tyranny, he lays part of the blame on the anarchic attitude towards social distinctions in a democracy, and mentions not only the lack of respect for parents among the younger generation but the fact that metics and citizens are put on a par (ἐξισοῦσθαι, 563a). Adeimantus offers no objection to this analysis.

It was in public life that a well-born or wealthy Athenian typically gained the respect of his peers; it was there that he shared in the honours of the state. Few would renounce such opportunities voluntarily, and rich metics did not. They did not withdraw from public life; they were simply not admitted to it. This was the price they paid for the privilege of living in Athenian society.

But there was another important social group at Athens whose aloofness from public life was enforced rather than voluntary: those members of the elite who preferred oligarchic to democratic ways, and who reacted against the influence of the lower orders in politics - if they were not among those few who sought actively to impose an oligarchy - by holding back from participation in public life. 'Quietism', ἀπραγμοσύνη, was a watchword among those whom wealth and birth made prominent. It sheltered them from the hostility of the people, who in litigious Athens had many means by which to make their hostility felt. But quietism was a choice made under pressure. Those who adopted it were depriving themselves of something they would have regarded as their right.

Glaucon and Adeimantus are quietists, as we shall see, and their attitude has made them good companions for those highly-cultured sons of Cephalus, for all that their metic quietism is differently motivated. Xenophon in the *Memorabilia* (3.6) writes a scene in which the not-quite-twenty year old Glaucon is urged by Socrates to contain his impatience and not attempt to enter the political arena until he has learnt what is required to manage a city well. He had been making a fool of himself by speaking up in the Assembly despite his youth and inexperience. In conversation with Xenophon's Socrates he turns out to have no conception of the technical knowledge required to run a city. His education, excellent though it may be, is of an old-fashioned type, and he is old-fashioned enough to think it qualifies him for public office. In the *Republic* Adeimantus describes him as a 'man who loves to win', a φιλόνικος; but Socrates insists Glaucon is more cultured and sophisticated than the ambitious, honour-loving type with whom Adeimantus is tempted to compare him (548d-e).

Both brothers, indeed, are too cultured, too noble to seek honour regardless of its cost, however much they may believe themselves worthy of holding public office. They react to the corruption of their society not as their kinsmen did, by staging a coup, but by holding themselves aloof and cultivating their souls. Critias in Plato's dialogues is shown in the company of Charmides, in the company also of the distinguished foreign visitors Timaeus and Hermocrates, but never in the company of metics. The opening scene of the *Republic* suggests that Glaucon and Adeimantus took no more part in Critias' coup than did their brother.

Yet though their reaction to the political mire is nobler than that of their cousin, it remains a mere reaction nonetheless. Quietism is not a way of life; it is a retreat from a way of life. In Book 7 Socrates will ask Glaucon whether any life except the life of true philosophy has a contempt for public office, and Glaucon will emphatically deny it (521b). Yet he is not himself living that life, for all that he is a sympathetic companion of Socrates and familiar with the talk of intellectuals. Much of what Socrates has to say he finds very surprising. Besides, we shall see soon enough the step that the brothers must take, and have not yet taken, if they are to live the philosophic life.

So it is not that Glaucon and Adeimantus have a contempt for public office; rather, they have withdrawn from it. Certainly they do their duty, and fight in Athens' wars (368a). But they are spending their time in cultured leisure, with fellow quietists. Yet if they count metics among their peers, this alone indicates that they are ready for something radical, something unconstrained by aristocratic reserve; for metics are not their peers in status, only in merit. They regard the sons of Cephalus as their own kind. But this attitude takes them down to the Piraeus, to the harbour, home for resident aliens who were not permitted to own property in the city of Athens and first port of call for everything strange and socially unsettling (compare *Laws* 704d-705b). It takes them to watch a novel type of torch-race in honour of a goddess newly-imported from Thrace (327a, 328a).

And here they will learn from Socrates of a society ruled by an aristocracy of merit, a society where all are citizens and none is alien, and where each citizen, fulfilling the dictates of civic justice, follows a maxim that in this society at least, and at last, translates as 'doing one's own job and not trying to do other people's jobs for them' (τὰ αὑτοῦ πράττειν καὶ μὴ πολυπραγμονεῖν, 433a). But in Glaucon's and Adeimantus' Athens that maxim means something different - two things, in fact, depending on whether it is addressed to the elite or to the common citizens. To the members of the elite it offers advice: Be a quietist, do not become involved in politics. To the common citizens it offers a warning: Know your place, do not attempt to usurp the authority of your betters. And it is because that warning went unheard in democratic Athens that the corresponding advice seemed good.

In Callipolis everyone does his own job, everyone minds his own business, is in that sense ἀπράγμων; but no one has to retreat from a full civic life. And in the vision of Callipolis Glaucon and Adeimantus will find a way to reconnect themselves happily to the prospect of public office - indeed, of kingship.

2. The values of a gentleman

Let us begin with the brothers' most extended contribution to the discussion, their set-piece speeches in Book 2, which resurrect Thrasymachus' argument that justice is a mug's game.

If Glaucon is to be truly persuaded that it is better to be just than unjust, he must first get a proper explanation, he says, of what justice and injustice are (357a, 358b). This much seems borrowed from Socrates' own complaint against himself at the end of Book 1, that he had moved on to the argument that justice was more profitable than injustice before settling what justice is. But Glaucon immediately goes further:

> As far as I'm concerned, the proof is not yet convincing, either for justice or injustice. I want to be told what each of them is, *and what power it has, just by itself* (αὐτὸ καθ' αὑτό), *when it is present in the soul*. (358b)

If Socrates could tell him this, he would in effect be praising justice αὐτὸ καθ' αὑτό, 'just by itself' (358d).

The phrase is, of course, the one that Socrates is in the habit of applying to those objects of knowledge that the philosopher strives to understand - justice itself, beauty itself, the good itself - in a quest that distinguishes his from the common run of human curiosity. Likewise, Glaucon is here asking for the deepest account of justice that he can imagine. He wants an account that praises the effects of justice within the individual and disregards the rewards and the reputation that it will elicit for the individual from others who regard him as just (358b). To strive for *this* sort of justice is to set oneself apart from 'the common run' (τοῖς πολλοῖς, 358a), for whom justice is a tiresome matter of conforming to social norms, often against one's inclination, and only worth doing for its material rewards and for the benefits of respectability.

There is an element of *hauteur* in Glaucon's disparagement of this attitude towards justice. To speak of material 'rewards', μισθοί, as a goal of 'the many', οἱ πολλοί, as Glaucon does (358a), is to suggest familiar complaints against the have-nots of Athens, who expect 'payment for public service' (μισθός), service that a gentleman performs, if circumstances allow, by virtue of his station. The second goal of the many, respectability, is expressed in terms suggestive of popular opinion and its pressures - εὐδοκιμήσεις, δόξα - rather than of aristocratic distinction. The class of good to which justice is consigned when regarded in this fashion is the ἐπίπονον εἶδος (358a)- not only 'painful' but 'tiresome' and 'laborious'. It is a class that Glaucon takes to include not only the painful process of being cured when sick but just as much the 'commercial activity' (χρηματισμός) of the doctor hired to administer the cure.

Glaucon's *hauteur* is also reflected in his threefold classification of goods, among which this tiresome class appears. He distinguishes goods by appeal to how we value them: some we value not for their consequences but for their own sake, others both for their own sake and for their consequences, yet others - this is the tiresome class - for their consequences only, and not at all for their own sake. The classification has provoked lively debate among modern scholars, both for its philosophic generality and for its apparent relevance to the issues at stake in modern moral philosophy between deontological and consequentialist theories. But if Plato intended the classification to bear such philosophic weight, would he have assigned it to Glaucon rather than to Socrates? And would he have allowed it to remain the one-off in the dialogues that it is?

If any classification of goods could be picked out as dominant in the dialogues, it would be that which divides goods of the soul from bodily and social goods (e.g. *Apology* 29d, *Phaedo* 68c, *Laws* 697b). Also prominent is the distinction between what we pursue as means and what we pursue as ends (e.g. *Lysis* 220a-b, *Gorgias* 467c), a distinction that roughly corresponds to what we find in Glaucon's account of the tiresome kind of good. Glaucon distinguishes the activity classed as good - receiving medical treatment when sick, for example - from its reward or beneficial consequence - cure. Health is the goal, it would seem, and medical treatment the means to achieve it. This is how the medical example is described in the passage just cited from the *Gorgias*, which adds that what we really desire is not the means but the end. Likewise the passage from the *Lysis* explains that the only truly valuable thing is not that which we acquire for the sake of something else, but that for the sake of which other things are acquired.

But on this point Glaucon's analysis is significantly different. It is what occupies the role of means rather than end that he classifies as good, even though these things are tiresome. Exercising one's body, receiving medical treatment, administering such treatment in order to earn a living - 'these activities, we would say, are tiresome but beneficial to us' (ἐπίπονα φαῖμεν ἄν, ὠφελεῖν δὲ ἡμᾶς, 357c). These are the items listed as belonging to the third class of good (τρίτον... εἶδος ἀγαθοῦ, ἐν ᾧ τό γυμνάζεσθαι...), while what occupies the role of end or goal is described rather as their 'wages', 'rewards' (μισθοί) or 'consequences' (ὅσα γίγνεται ἀπ' αὐτῶν).

All three of Glaucon's examples of the third type of good, we should note, are processes that lead to health. Being healthy, however, he mentions not in this third category but as an example in the second category of good, those which are valued both for their own sake and for their consequences. He ranges it with the examples of thinking and seeing. This serves to emphasize that the second category is not simply a combination of the first and third.

One might suppose that if the first group comprises things valued for their own sake and the third things valued for their consequences, then the second, comprising as it does things valued both for their own sake and for their consequences, combines these two modes of valuation. (Aristotle's comparable classification in the first book of the *Nicomachean Ethics,* 1097a15-b6, treats the modes of valuation in this way.) But the third category does not after all comprise everything that is valued for its consequences; rather it comprises things that, taken in themselves, are painful or tiresome, and that we therefore cannot desire except for their consequences. Goods of the second category are not, in other words, goods of the third category that also, lucky things, are desirable in their own right. It is important that goods of Glaucon's third type are not just neutral means to desirable consequences but are a tiresome effort that we would avoid if we could. A person who pursues health as the reward of a good of the third kind is treating health differently from one who ranks it in the second category.

The effect of Glaucon's classification, by contrast with an analysis that designates health as the goal and as the good at which we aim by means of gymnastics, medicine, or whatever, is this. Pursuing ends by means is demoted to the rank of a tiresome and laborious category of good, a businessman's category of good. Being healthy, and other goods of the second group, are seen not as rewards acquired as the result of effort but as conditions valuable in themselves, conditions which stand not at the end but at the origin of other goods, their consequences, but which would remain valuable even apart from those consequences.

It is a cultured aristocrat's classification of goods. Thinking, seeing, being healthy, the condition of a human being in the fullness of his powers - this we can welcome for its own sake, independently of our regard for the benefits those powers can bring. 'Thinking, seeing, being healthy' (τὸ φρονεῖν καὶ τὸ ὁρᾶν καὶ τὸ ὑγιαίνειν); not intelligence, sight, health, which would fit the most common, even if not universal, pattern of those lists of conventional goods that appear elsewhere in the dialogues.[1] Glaucon's goods, in all categories, are expressed as states or activities or processes. Not pleasure, but 'being pleased' (τὸ χαίρειν, 357b); not 'gymnastics', not 'the art of medicine' (γυμναστική, ἰατρική) but 'taking exercise', 'doctoring' (τὸ γυμνάζεσθαι, ἰάτρευσις, 357c).

The effect is, again, to emphasize states or activities over achievements. 'Health' (ὑγίεια) is something we seek to achieve, the goal of those caught up in the tiresome business of doctoring and being doctored; 'being healthy' (τὸ ὑγιαίνειν) is the condition of those who do not need to struggle, whether to make money or to counteract the damage done to health by hard labour or poor diet. And it is those who do not need to struggle, those born to excellent conditions, who can afford to benefit themselves and their fellow-citizens with the goods that flow from their superiority. Glaucon would perhaps have chosen to emphasise achievements more, had his city not confined him to states or activities.

This is not, I should make clear, a point of grammar; τὸ ὑγιαίνειν and other infinitives used as nouns can designate goals in Plato. Our passage about means and ends from the *Gorgias* (467c) contains an example. The point derives rather from Glaucon's usage in the passage as a whole. It is a literary point.

[1] E.g. *Protagoras* 341b, 354b, *Gorgias* 467e, *Laws* 631c, and elsewhere in the *Republic* at 618b, d.

If it seems unlikely that a Greek aristocrat would demote physical exercise to a low grade of good - isn't it to the gymnasia of Athens that Socrates goes when looking for his aristocratic young companions? - the qualm can be dispelled by considering how Herodicus is criticized later in the *Republic*. Herodicus, says Socrates at 406a, was a gym-trainer who became an invalid, and reacted by 'mixing gymnastics with the doctor's art' (μείξας γυμναστικὴν ἰατρικῇ). This was an error; his hypochondria succeeded only in spoiling the rest of his life and the lives of those around him. 'A fine prize he won for his skill' (καλὸν ἄρα τὸ γέρας τῆς τέχνης ἠνέγκατο), comments Glaucon, using a word for 'prize' (γέρας) that carries aristocratic associations of privilege and glory. The gentleman does not take physical exercise for the sake of his health; he does not mix gymnastics with doctoring. He takes his exercise as an expression of cultivated leisure (compare *Protagoras* 312b). He may also, indeed, bring glory on himself and on his city by engaging in athletic competition. But this does not, or should not, turn physical exercise into a means directed at an end. Athletic competition remained even under democracy a redoubt of aristocratic excellence. One competed not for financial reward, at least not primarily, but for the glory symbolized by a simple wreath of laurel. The glory of victory crowned one's pre-existing worth.

The aristocratic flavour of Glaucon's classification is enhanced in several ways by the subsequent remarks of his brother Adeimantus. Most importantly, he is explicit about which aspect of those goods that we value both for their own sake and for their consequences carries more weight. This second category of good, it has been agreed, is the most important (367c, and compare 358a). But Adeimantus insists that what we value most within this most important category is the thing itself rather than its consequences:

> those greatest goods which are worth having for their consequences, but much more so (πολὺ δὲ μᾶλλον) for their own sake, goods such as seeing, hearing, thinking, and being healthy too (οἷον ὁρᾶν, ἀκούειν, φρονεῖν, καὶ ὑγιαίνειν δή), and the rest of that true-blue class which are good by their very nature, and not because of the reputation they bring (καὶ ὅσ' ἄλλα ἀγαθὰ γόνιμα τῇ αὐτῶν φύσει ἀλλ' οὐ δόξῃ ἐστίν). (367c-d)

We are not to focus on consequences; we are not striving after achievement. If these goods are 'worth having for their consequences', that is, 'worth having obtained' (ἄξια κεκτῆσθαι), this would be because we are already possessed of them. Where Glaucon asks Socrates to show him what effect justice has just by itself within the soul (358b), Adeimantus asks him to show

19

what effect justice has just by itself 'on the person who possesses it' (τὸν ἔχοντα, 367b, d, e), or 'within the soul of the person who possesses it' (τῇ τοῦ ἔχοντος ψυχῇ ἐνόν, 366e). If Socrates can do this, he will have placed justice among the 'true-blue', 'blue-blooded' goods (γόνιμα), those which are suited to the gentleman whose excellent attributes and leisurely pursuits are worthwhile in themselves, and only secondarily render him an ornament to his city, should his city allow it. (Interpretations divide over the meaning of the word γόνιμα, but whether it is understood as 'true-blue' or as 'fertile', it retains associations with good breeding.)

Towards the end of his speech, Adeimantus introduces a potent image into the discussion. He suggests at 367a that if it could be shown that injustice is the worst evil a soul can have within itself, and justice the greatest good, then each of us would be his own best 'guardian' (φύλαξ), fearing that to commit injustice would be to 'dwell with the greatest of evils' (τῷ μεγίστῳ κακῷ σύνοικος ᾖ), admit it into the place where *he* is to be found, his soul.

Self-guardianship, as Adeimantus presents it, is a metaphor well matched to the *hauteur* of his brother's contribution. The guardian of himself is motivated by fear of the harm he could inflict on himself, rather than by fear of the harm that others could inflict on him (οὐκ ἂν ἀλλήλους ἐφυλάττομεν μὴ ἀδικεῖν, 367a). He is self-contained. What is more, that self-containment is represented as a refusal to be contained by society. It is a retreat from watching out for what others could do to you - that is, what harm they could do to you - but it is by the same token a retreat from watching out for others, from watching over them, as guardian rather than guard. The words φυλάττειν and φύλαξ are capable of the same ambiguities as the English here. Instead of watching against and over others one will watch against and over oneself, impose discipline on the potentially recalcitrant elements within.

Adeimantus' is a counsel of quietism and thereby of individual, gentlemanly perfection in an imperfect world. For even though a self that must be watched against and over is a self that contains inferior elements, the person who can control those elements within himself is uncontaminated by them. He does not 'dwell with evil' (κακῷ σύνοικος); within the society of his soul, at least, even if not in the democracy that surrounds him, inferior elements know their place. It is a society where all is well.

3. Why govern?

There is an obvious objection to this account of Glaucon and Adeimantus as gentlemen who do not strive after achievement, and this is that readers of the *Republic* are likely to come away with the feeling that these are as spirited and competitive a pair of characters as any in the dialogues. What is more, it has become a scholarly commonplace to describe Greek culture as unusually competitive, at least among the members of its elite. Nor is praise for the rewards of 'exertion', πόνος, absent from the values of that elite. To strive for undying fame was what the best sort of person was typically thought to do, as Diotima reminds Socrates in the *Symposium* (208c-d).

For Glaucon, although not for Adeimantus, the dialogue provides epithets that characterize him explicitly, and which support the judgment that he is competitive. His refusal to accept Thrasymachus' surrender earns him the description 'very bold' (ἀνδρειότατος, 357a), a word that retains the connotation 'very manly'. This is only the first of several determined interventions and objections on Glaucon's part, one of them described by Socrates as a sudden assault (472a); so it comes as no surprise that Adeimantus will later attribute 'love of victory' to him (φιλονικία, 548d). These traits find expression in more than the battle of words, for Glaucon is a warhero. At 368a Socrates quotes a line from a poem written by Glaucon's lover to celebrate his distinguishing himself at the battle of Megara.

But the poem is addressed also to Adeimantus, who distinguished himself alongside his brother. Adeimantus is no less willing than his brother to offer determined resistance in the course of discussion (e.g. 419a, 449b-c, 487b). Nor does he lack the spirit of competition: not only does he begin his long speech in Book 2 by suggesting that it will cap rather than merely supplement Glaucon's ('The part that most needs to be included has been left out', 362d), but his very attribution of competitiveness to his brother feels like a gratuitous dig, if a playful one. Certainly there was no need to mention Glaucon at this point, where the discussion is of types rather than particular persons (548d).

If the brothers are indeed competitive, if they are achievers after all, why do they insist in chorus that Socrates give them an account of justice shorn of its prizes, honours, and rewards? For all that aristocratic achievement was distinct from mere labour and participated in a rhetoric of freedom and leisure that softened its aspect of hard striving, the brothers' determined rejection of prizes still stands out. Are they struggling against their own competitive nature, then? No: they are expressing it. They set their value too high to compete in an arena that is unworthy of them. They are achievers, all right; but they wish to achieve by having the world recognize their inherent worth. It is not their place to work for the world's regard. In its absence, the satisfaction of self-regard will have to suffice. Blame the uselessness of the worthiest men on those who fail to use them, Socrates says in Book 6 (489b). And there he employs terms reminiscent of the political debate over quietism and of Pericles' accusation in Thucydides (2.40.2) that the so-called 'quietist' (ἀπράγμων) was merely 'useless' (ἀχρεῖος). Socrates applies these terms not to aristocrats, however, but to the philosophers.

Socrates' task will be to deflect the brothers from the feeling that quietism is the best recourse in their imperfect world. It is a task foreshadowed by a revealing moment of bafflement that Glaucon experiences in Book 1. Socrates is refuting Thrasymachus' challenge, the challenge that Glaucon will renew in Book 2. In the course of arguing that justice is a mug's game, Thrasymachus had claimed that those in government invariably draft laws with a view to the advantage of their class rather than for the common good. Socrates disputes this. In fact, no one goes into government of his own accord (346e). Why would anyone want to get involved and share in other people's troubles by attempting to put them right? No, if one is to consent to rule, some 'reward' or 'payment' (μισθόν), either money or prestige, must be on offer; either this, or a penalty for not ruling.

Here Glaucon intervenes. He is familiar with the two kinds of payment that Socrates has mentioned, 'but the penalty you refer to, and how you can put it in the category of a payment, that I don't understand'. Socrates' reply is of a sort to arouse Glaucon's emulousness: Then you don't understand the payment that makes the 'best' people, the 'most capable' people, consent to rule, he retorts - using terms with strong implications of social rank, οἱ βέλτιστοι, οἱ ἐπιεικέστατοι. (Imagine how Glaucon feels hearing this!) Don't you know, he continues, that 'ambition and greed' (τὸ φιλότιμόν τε καὶ φιλάργυρον) are regarded as, and indeed are, things to be ashamed of? Glaucon makes up for his earlier lapse with a decided response: 'I surely do' ("Εγωγε).

Now, if 'love of money', φιλαργυρία, was regularly the object of social opprobrium, φιλοτιμία - 'a passion for honour'? or mere 'ambition'? - was regarded with far more ambivalence. As Kenneth Dover has documented, its range of meaning includes, at the negative pole, aggressive self-assertion and social display, but at the positive, the desire to earn respect, especially for public service; indeed, Dover suggests 'patriotism' as the appropriate translation in many of the positive cases.[2]

If Glaucon is quite confident that τὸ φιλότιμον is not only regarded as but actually is something to be ashamed of, his attitude goes beyond convention - for convention would dictate less confidence over the matter - and enters the territory of quietism. If there is some motive that the best people have for ruling and Glaucon has not heard of it yet, he most certainly wants to hear of it now, because he considers himself one of the best people, and has done his share of thinking about the conditions under which one would seek a political career. That is why he cannot resist breaking in on Socrates' discussion with Thrasymachus, and why he can claim to be 'familiar with the two kinds of payment you mention' (τοὺς μὲν γὰρ δύο μισθοὺς γιγνώσκω). Glaucon is ambitious, but his reflections on political ambition - perhaps in combination with some experiences of the type that Xenophon portrays - have caused him to retreat within his shell. Yet Socrates seems aware that the interest and the ambition persist, ready to be rekindled by a strong enough flame.

The way is clear for Socrates to offer Glaucon a most unusual motive for going into government. Good people do not go into government for the money; for they neither want 'to be called' (κεκλῆσθαι) mercenary if they make money openly, nor be called thieves if they make it secretly (347b). Nor do they go into government for the sake of prestige. Why not? Simply because 'they are not lovers of prestige', 'not ambitious' (οὐ γάρ εἰσι φιλότιμοι). Socrates does not say, in this case, that they do not wish *to be called* ambitious, despite saying they did not wish to be called mercenary, or be called thieves; and this even though ambition, no less than greed, is something that he had claimed not only 'is' but '*is said to be*' shameful (λέγεταί τε καὶ ἔστιν).

There is an asymmetry among the desires of the good. Money is not something to which they are indifferent. (Even Socrates, after all, prays in the final

---

2 Dover 1994 (1974), 229-34.

lines of the *Phaedrus* for just so much gold as a moderate man can cope with.) It is not because they do not want money that they would avoid politics but because they do not wish to lose their reputation as good people. They do not want to be called mercenary, or to be called thieves; and if you make money as a politician you will very likely be called both. Political life in a democracy is dangerous to one's reputation; that was one reason for aristocratic quietism. But prestige, that is, the prestige that comes from living in the public eye and occupying a position of power in society: to this the good are truly indifferent. It is not that they do not want *to be called* ambitious; it is rather that, being good, they simply are not ambitious. Being good, and being regarded as good, is for them quite good enough.

Lacking the normal incentives for taking up political power, good people must be compelled by a penalty if they decline to do so; and that penalty consists in being ruled by one's inferiors (347c). Fearing this, and not having betters or even equals to whom they could delegate the job, they consent to govern, regarding the task 'as something they cannot avoid but not as something good' (οὐχ ὡς ἐπ' ἀγαθόν τι ἰόντες... ἀλλ' ὡς ἐπ' ἀναγκαῖον), nor as something which will 'bring them personal benefit or pleasure' (οὐδ'ὡς εὐπαθήσοντες ἐν αὐτῷ). Were there a city made up entirely of good men, Socrates imagines that they would struggle to *avoid* having to rule with as much passion as men now struggle for the opportunity to rule. Each would choose to let someone else do good to him, rather than involve himself in the complicated business of doing good to others (347d).

Judged by the standards of the society that Socrates and Glaucon shared, this is a peculiar motivation for a superior sort of person to have. Aristotle in the *Nicomachean Ethics* expresses something closer to the norm when he describes the person who is conscious of his own superiority, the μεγαλόψυχος or 'great-souled' man, as one who would do good to others but be ashamed to have good done to him, since doing good is proper to the superior person, and receiving it to the inferior (1124b9-10). This motivation, so far from vanishing or being turned into its opposite when he is among his equals, is only increased: the greater the status and reputation of the person he does favours for, the more difficult and impressive is his display of superiority (1124b17-23). A person whose motivation for ruling is so dependent on a sense of his own worth and dignity would not suddenly lose this sense of himself when among his peers.

Against such a background, it becomes clear that Socrates has seized upon an ordinary social fact and given a quite abnormal explanation of it. Here is the social fact: 'It has always been regarded as a disgrace for people to seek office voluntarily, rather than waiting until they are forced to seek it' (347c). Socrates offers his account of the motives of good people as a hypothesis that would explain this widespread attitude: 'That's probably why it has always been regarded as a disgrace... (ὅθεν κινδυνεύει... αἰσχρὸν νενομίσθαι)'. The tentativeness of his proposal is well advised. In a society that cannot decide whether political ambition is good or bad but wants to have it both ways, the obvious reason for disapproving of those who seek out public office is not, as Socrates claims, that good people are not politically ambitious, but that they do not want to be called politically ambitious, and should not invite that reputation. You must not be too openly ambitious if you wish to fulfil your ambitions; a modest and decent reluctance will be more likely to secure the encouragement and approval that self-promotion would deter.

It is not difficult to see that through Socrates' extraordinary analysis Plato is planting the idea that will come to fruit in Callipolis and its government made up of philosophers. The good people who are not politically ambitious are not the 'best men' of Athens but philosophers, the elite of a hypothetical city. Not that Callipolis, however, is the city made up of good men in which each vies with the other not to rule. Such a city is yet more hypothetical than Callipolis, for it would be a self-sufficient community consisting entirely of philosophers. In Callipolis, philosophers live together with those who are not philosophers, on whom they depend for sustenance. Although these providers are not up to the philosophic mark, they are an essential element of the community. So those who contemplate Callipolis cannot escape the question whether superior or inferior will rule, and what will motivate the superior to do so.

4. A real man

In Book 1, Glaucon does not get the chance to react to Socrates' analysis of what motivates the good man to enter government. Socrates postpones examination of the issue (347d-e), and it is not until he introduces philosopher-kings into the argument that it becomes clear what he has in mind.

But the response that Glaucon might have given in Book 1 emerges sooner than this, when he renews Thrasymachus' argument in Book 2. Describing the view of justice that he will defend, but defend only on condition that Socrates can give him the arguments with which to reject it - the view that he has disparaged as that of the common run - he asserts that those who practise justice do so unwillingly, 'regarding it as something unavoidable, not as something good' (ἄκοντες ἐπιτηδεύουσιν ὡς ἀναγκαῖον ἀλλ' οὐχ ὡς ἀγαθόν, 358c). But these were almost exactly the terms in which Socrates expressed the superior person's attitude towards the task of assuring just government. Glaucon, a superior person himself, evidently has reservations about this attitude. Socrates will have to go further if he is to draw Glaucon out of his shell.

What is more, the reservations that he goes on to express - he the ἀνδρειότατος, 'most virile' Glaucon - are presented as those of the real man, the manly man. Where Thrasymachus had described his superior person simply as one who could turn 'the law', νόμος, to his own advantage, Glaucon conceives the law as a restriction on 'nature', φύσις, that is, on a natural desire to thrust oneself forward by taking advantage of others (πεφυκέναι, φύσις 358e, 359b, c).

It seems likely, as Mario Vegetti has argued[3] that he is borrowing the argument from Antiphon, who was both an intellectual and - a fact more pertinent to the concerns of this chapter - an oligarchic revolutionary who had previously been a quietist. Thucydides (8.68.1) tells us that his reputation for cleverness did not go down well with the public, and this caused him to keep a low profile. A 'real man' (ὡς ἀληθῶς ἄνδρα, 359b), says Glaucon, would never agree to the feeble compromise of a social contract not to wrong others if they will not wrong you - here echoing Antiphon's description of the social contract. This would make no sense, because, Glaucon implies, he would have the strength and the boldness to succeed without its help. The basis of such a contract is weakness and fear - fear of being wronged by the stronger (compare 360d).

[3] Vegetti, ed. 1998 [vol. 2], 163-69.

All of this, of course, is what others, not Glaucon, say - as Glaucon repeatedly insists (358c, 359b, 361e). But Socrates has his doubts, and so should we. Looking back on both Glaucon's and Adeimantus' speeches, he admits that were he judging from their speeches alone rather than from their character and honourable record, he would scarcely believe that they had not in fact been persuaded that injustice was superior to justice (368a).

To derive justice from a contract of this sort is to regard it as a good thing only by way of its rewards - that is, the reward of not suffering wrong. And Glaucon's contempt for the view that justice is a good thing only by way of its rewards is genuine. We saw him voice it in his own name, before launching into his devil's advocacy (358a). If he imagines that a 'real man' would trample on the terms of such a contract, that real man is close to his own heart. He complains that he has never heard justice praised in the way he would like, praised for itself (358d); but he has certainly heard it *denounced* in a way he likes - denounced as an expedient for the feeble and the lazy. Having withdrawn from a politics that panders to the feeble and the lazy of democratic Athens, he and his brother have withdrawn also from the social domain in which the virtue of justice is conventionally active. But they have not despaired of justice. What they want to hear now from Socrates is a proof that the quietist is a just man too, indeed, the most just of men. They are not so interested in the proof that justice beats injustice; they are already confident that it does (347e). What they want is a new account of justice that fits with the path of withdrawal and self-containment that they have chosen (358b, 367b, e).

The lack of such an account is one of the points that Adeimantus brings to our attention, when he begins his speech by insisting that we must consider what sorts of arguments people typically use to *recommend* justice, rather than to condemn it, if we are to understand what Glaucon has in mind (362e). Those arguments *in favour of* justice then turn out to have the very same structure as the ones that Glaucon brought *against* justice. So it is small wonder that he is in search of a more effective argument to enlist on justice's side.

Parents and poets expatiate on the rewards that await the law-abiding man in this life and the next (363a-e), says Adeimantus. Compare how Glaucon described the security - the freedom from criminal harm - that rewards those who accept the restrictions of law. Parents and poets declare with one voice that justice is a good, a 'fine' thing (καλόν, 364a), yet 'laborious' or

27

'painful' (ἐπίπονον) and liable to bring less success in the world than injustice, which is shameful only by 'convention' (νόμῳ). Besides, the risks and opprobrium that attend injustice can be evaded or expunged from the record by various well-established devices. Likewise, Glaucon's speech located justice in the third class of goods, the 'laborious' or 'painful' class (ἐπίπονον εἶδος), and he made its pursuit contingent on public regard. Who among us, he asked, could chance upon a ring of invisibility and not be corrupted? Those who have the wherewithal to escape public disapproval of any misbehaviour will duly indulge themselves. In this they will be obeying a natural bent and ignoring social convention (359c).

That is why George Grote is only technically correct when he complains that Socrates should not have represented Glaucon and Adeimantus' speeches as defamations of justice, when in fact they were giving arguments showing that justice is indeed a good, even if a good of the third class - good for what results from it rather than good in itself,[4] Socrates heard right. Glaucon has a general disdain for goods of the third class. He believes that justice has no place among them.

5. The values of a philosopher

Yet by the time we get to Book 7, and to Socrates' account of why the philosopher-king will consent to return to the Cave and govern in the city of his upbringing, Glaucon has undergone something of a conversion. Will they disobey us, these people we have brought up, asks Socrates (520d)? Will they refuse to 'do their share' of the city's 'labours' (συμπονεῖν)? Impossible, Glaucon replies, and volunteers both an explanation and a caveat:

> They can't possibly refuse. It's a just demand, and they are just people. But they will undoubtedly appoach ruling, each one of them, as something unavoidable (ἀναγκαῖον) - just the opposite of the people who rule in every city at the moment.

Socrates agrees, and in his summation at the end of Book 7 (540b) makes still more explicit than Glaucon did the correspondence with his account in Book 1 of what would motivate good people to go into government. Philosopher-kings will take their turn at ruling 'for the city's sake,

---

[4] Grote 1885 [vol. 4], 117.

regarding what they do not not as a fine but as a necessary thing' (τῆς πόλεως ἕνεκα, οὐχ ὡς καλόν τι ἀλλ' ὡς ἀναγκαῖον πράττοντας) - just as the good people of Book 1 approached the task 'not as a good but as something unavoidable' (οὐχ ὡς ἐπ' ἀγαθόν τι ἰόντες... ἀλλ'ὡς ἐπ' ἀναγκαῖον, 347d). This time round, Glaucon is allowed to respond, and his response is enthusiastic: 'What fine, fine men (παγκάλους) you have fashioned as your rulers, Socrates!'

What can it be that in the interim has made Glaucon willing to accept such an account of the just society, to find admirable those who take up the task of maintaining its justice in a spirit so similar to that which he found contemptible among the common run of people who practice justice 'against their will, regarding it as unavoidable rather than as good' (ἄκοντες... ὡς ἀναγκαῖον ἀλλ'οὐχ ὡς ἀγαθόν, 358c)?

What has happened is that Socrates has given the most manly Glaucon a new kind of model to measure himself against: the philosopher-king, who is not only a philosopher but also a 'real man', sprung from the warrior class, and who disparages no less than Glaucon does conformity to social norms for the sake of merely social success. If he has no need to retreat to quietism and self-guardianship as Glaucon and Adeimantus have done, that would be for two reasons: because he lives in a society where success is worthwhile, and because his ultimate goal lies beyond human society altogether.

The philosopher, being just, obediently takes up the just task assigned to him, doing it 'for the sake of the city', and considering it 'necessary' - 'necessary' if the city is to be free from conflict (520c-d). 'Necessary' rather than 'unavoidable', because he is considering what means are necessary to achieve a certain aim. In that sense, the philosopher, unlike the common run of people, does not after all pursue justice 'unwillingly', ἄκων; for he would not avoid ruling, not in Callipolis (592a), even if he could get away with it. The common man, Glaucon thought, would indeed avoid the demands of justice if he had a ring of invisibility. The unwillingness with which justice is pursued when it is pursued as a good of Glaucon's third class had been Glaucon's addition to this theme. It turns out to be the element in it that he finds most objectionable. Once he has been shown how a person need not be unwilling to pursue a justice that he regards as necessary but not as something fine or noble - once he has seen how this attitude can belong to a 'fine' or 'noble' person (πάγκαλος) - he takes it up with enthusiasm.

Yet what is not unwillingly pursued can still be regarded with reserve. The philosopher-king's attitude to ruling differs from that of the good people described in Book 1 not so much in the enthusiasm with which he approaches the task as in the fact that, where they do not regard public office as 'good', ἀγαθόν, he does not regard it as 'fine' or 'noble', καλόν. Ruling a good society like Callipolis is a different proposition from taking up public office amid the typical corruption of an average society. Yet even so, the philosopher-king cannot regard his kingly task as something καλόν, cannot glory in it; and the reason he cannot glory in it is that he has justice at work within his soul, and it is a truer justice, as we shall see, than is at work in the city. It would seem to be exactly what Glaucon and Adeimantus asked for when they wanted to be told what effect justice has, by itself, when present in the soul.

Despite appearances, however, Socrates is giving the brothers more than they requested. I mean this not in the obvious sense that he arrives at his answer about the completely just person's soul by way of an elaborate description of the completely just society. I mean rather that his emphasis on the individual soul, his argument that justice is primarily to be found not within society but within the soul (443c-d), has a different intention and expresses a different ethos than Glaucon's and Adeimantus' apparently similar assignment of priorities.

Adeimantus' hope that each person could be educated to become his own best guardian (367a) was, we saw, a counsel of gentlemanly perfection. He who is guardian of himself lives uncontaminated by the inferior elements within. Glaucon, for his part, fears that unless we strip the just man of all prizes and recognition, it will be unclear whether the only reason he acts justly is for their sake (361c). How vigorously you 'cleanse' him (ἐκκαθαίρεις)! remarks Socrates. 'As if you were scouring a statue!' (361d). Glaucon's paragon of justice, like Adeimantus', is completely pure; and because of his purity, his virtue shines out. It gleams like a freshly cleaned statue.

True, Glaucon is also polishing the statue of the perfectly *un*just man to the same gleaming finish. But what both brothers need to learn is that no human soul can be completely pure or for that matter completely impure.

The philosopher, like the gentleman, takes seriously the task of maintaining good order among the superior and inferior elements of his soul. The inner politics of both men is a conservative politics of εὐνομία, of 'law and order'. Where the philosopher differs from the gentleman is in not regarding that politics as pure. The gentleman supposes that within himself he has found an escape from the impure politics of the society in which he lives. But the philosopher is capable of regarding even the task of arranging the politics of his soul as a necessity, not as something glorious, just as he thinks it a necessity, not something glorious, that philosophers should rule, and notwithstanding the fact that justice amounts to something more in his soul than it does in the city. (This fact will return for fuller consideration in chapter 4.)

If philosophic rule is a necessity imposed on the philosopher by the particular circumstances of his birth, breeding, and education (520b), politics of the soul is imposed on him by his very humanity. As the *Republic* comes to a close, Glaucon and Adeimantus will learn that the soul cannot become 'pure' (καθαρόν, 611c), cannot be cleansed, until it is free of its association with the human body and the effects of a human life, an association that maims and disfigures it as if it had been cast in the sea and become encrusted with barnacles and weeds (611c-612a). Only death can set it free.

To be sure, the virtuous soul, the soul whose politics is well conducted, is healthy rather than diseased (444d-e). For most of the discussion it is this view of the soul that prevails, and only at the end does Socrates state outright how even the healthy human soul appears from the cosmic perspective. Yet this perspective has been operative throughout, for it has been a determinant of the philosopher's behaviour (e.g. 484c, 486a, 520c). To be healthy of soul is not yet to be pure of soul. Health is a means to the goal of purity. Socrates prepares the ground for this thought by implicitly correcting Glaucon's and Adeimantus' view of bodily health, which they had assigned to the class of things good for their own sake as well as for their consequences (357c, 367d).

Health of the body, he explains in a climactic analysis of the task of conducting the soul's politics, at the end of Book 9, is not to be valued except to the extent that it helps with self-discipline. One should keep the body in balance for the sake of producing harmony in the soul (591c-d). The reader is thus prepared for the final turn of the screw in Book 10: health of the body is for the sake of the soul's health, and health of the soul is to be maintained, in turn, so that the soul's godlike part, its reason, can flourish and eventually be purified.

A double perspective is at work here; the philosopher takes both a human and a godlike view of human life. Philosophers are not gods; they have human lives to lead, and in those lives they will value their souls' justice for its own sake, together with the external benefits that their inner justice can win for them and for those around them. It is from this human perspective that Socrates agrees with Glaucon in Book 2 that justice belongs in the second class of goods - which he calls 'the finest class' (ἐν τῷ καλλίστῳ, 358a) - the class of things that are to be valued both for their own sake and for their consequences 'by anyone who is going to be happy' (τῷ μέλλοντι μακαρίῳ ἔσεσθαι). Life on the isles of the blest - contemplation of the forms - would if one could remain there and never return be a good of Glaucon's first type, good for its own sake, but without consequences; it would be a pleasure from which nothing results in time to come but the delightful condition itself (357b). Even the pleasures of soul enjoyed by the philosopher in his ordinary existence, after all, are unmixed with pain (583b-586e) - which is not to say that the philosopher's ordinary existence is itself unmixed with pain. But Glaucon himself never developed that first category of good, offered no example more definite than harmless pleasure and concentrated instead on the question whether justice was a good of his second or his third type. The *Republic* as a whole maintains Glaucon's emphasis.

It is from this human perspective too that Socrates will describe the external benefits of justice, including even those that accrue in the afterlife, as 'prizes' (ἆθλα, 608c, 613c, 614a). For in the *Republic* the divine remains always in the background, and the human is front and centre: 'As things stand,' says Socrates in retrospect, 'we have given an adequate description of the things that can happen to the soul, the shapes it can assume, in human life' (612a). Even the disembodied souls of the concluding myth are preoccupied with their reincarnation and the task of choosing another human life. From the human perspective, the benefits of the afterlife crown one's pre-existing worth as the wreath of laurel does the aristocratic competitor in the games (613c, 621d).

It is a perspective that philosophers share. As human beings, they will value health of the soul for its own sake, for what else can they do? They are only human. *Of course* it is simply good, if you are human, to be able to live in the fullness of your human capacities, to live with a healthy soul; *of course* you will welcome this for its own sake. I say 'of course', because it seems only natural to desire and delight in the exercise of one's natural capacities. But this is, to be sure, a high-minded construal of human capacities; these are not values that one must hold simply by virtue of being human. It is a human perspective that philosophers share with gentlemen of Glaucon's stamp, rather than with all men.

Glaucon is not wrong, then, when he announces at the end of Book 4 that a person's life is not going to be worth living 'when the natural constitution of the very thing by which he lives (τῆς δὲ αὐτοῦ τούτου ᾧ ζῶμεν φύσεως) is upset and ruined', so that it would be ridiculous to pursue any further the question whether injustice can be profitable, now that we have seen that this amounts to asking whether it can profit a man to live with the health of his soul ruined (445a-b). He is not wrong; nevertheless, Socrates does not allow him to bring the discussion to a halt. Yes, it is 'ridiculous' (γελοῖον), he concedes; but 'now that we've got to the point of being able to see as clearly as possible that this is how things are, this isn't the moment to take a rest' (445b).

What Socrates proceeds to allow Glaucon to see is that life's questions do not terminate in the health of the soul. The human soul, even a sleek and healthy, gleaming, beautiful human soul, whose health belongs to the most beautiful class of good (another meaning of ἐν τῷ καλλίστῳ, 358a), is not the be-all and end-all. You can still ask how justice profits a man, even after you have discovered that justice is health of the soul. If it is a ridiculous question, that would be because you cannot pursue it without adopting some very counter-intuitive proposals (452b-e, 473c-d), nor without astonishing your friends by assuring them that the soul is immortal (608d). If it is nevertheless a question worth pursuing, that would be because there remains a goal for the healthy soul to achieve. That goal is true blessedness - if I may wring the phrase μακαρίῳ ἔσεσθαι at 358a for its last drop of meaning - a goal which the healthy soul can touch (519c) but not fully attain in a human life (540b-c).

For if the philosopher can agree with the gentleman in finding the healthy human soul a thing of excellence and beauty, to be admired for its own sake, that is not simply because, like the gentleman, he is disposed to value what is excellent and beautiful - value it for its own sake more than for its consequences (367c). It is also because he strives to locate the

33

beauty of a healthy human soul within the beauty and order of the entire cosmos (486a). But this striving takes him to a perspective from which even the healthy human soul can seem disfigured with weeds and barnacles. To maintain natural order in what would otherwise be disordered is simply good, good in itself, because natural order is good in itself. Yet the need to maintain order is still cause for regret. Just because the philosopher is capable of finding 'beauty', κάλλος, in the order of the human soul does not mean that he finds 'glorious', καλόν, the task of maintaining that order.

The gentlemanly ethos, then, is not sufficient. There is a noble sort of profit-seeking, a pursuit of ends by laborious means that does not borrow from the ethos of the businessman. The instrument of this noble profit-seeking is an entire philosophic life. This is to take the godlike rather than the human view. It is to see the toil of human life through the lens of metaphors less glittering than the athletic sort: husbandry (589b), helmsmanship (591e). Maintaining order in one's soul is in this view a concession to necessity.

Sources and Scholarly Contexts for Chapter 1

For the general theme of aristocratic quietism, which I apply in this chapter to Glaucon and Adeimantus, I have relied on the stimulating account in Carter 1986, as well as on Donlan 1980. These studies are also among those which make a theme of competitive values among the elite. Scholarship on the position of striving and exertion within a gentlemanly lifestyle is taken up and developed in Johnstone 1994. Whitehead 1977 has proved an important resource for thinking about the situation of the metics at Athens.

It is within the tradition that descends from Leo Strauss' reading of the *Republic* (Strauss 1964, ch. 2) that one finds the fullest treatment of Glaucon and Adeimantus as characters. Elsewhere (Ferrari 1997) I have attempted to come to terms with that reading in some detail, and as a whole. The studies of the *Republic* within this tradition that I have consulted most are Bloom 1968, Benardete 1989, Brann 1989-90, Howland 1993, and Craig 1994. It is a theme of Strauss' reading that Socrates is offering a cure for political ambition, a cure of which Glaucon, at least, stands in need. In the interpretation that I offer here, political ambition is an issue on which both Glaucon and Adeimantus meet Socrates more than half-way. They have already withdrawn from the political maelstrom. Glaucon is not, or is no longer, the youngster whom me meet in the pages of Xenophon.

The tradition that makes Glaucon the focus of Socrates' attention tends also to rank him the intellectual superior of Adeimantus (Bloom 1968, pp. 344-46, Brann 1989-90, pp. 44-46, and above all Craig 1994, ch. 5.) Outside this tradition the widespread judgment that Glaucon has the sharper intellect may be connected with a difference in the brothers' interests but not, as in Bloom or Craig, with a difference in ethos. See for example Vegetti's study of Glaucon, Vegetti, ed. 1998 [vol. 2], pp. 151-172. (Vegetti also sees the brothers as potential tyrants, p. 153.) If I choose not to distinguish the brothers but to pair them as representatives of a single ethos, it is not because I do not think there are distinctions between them that could repay attention.

I have not hesitated to use the *Seventh Letter* when associating the reign of the Thirty with the themes of this chapter; but this is not to claim that the letter is authentic. One may well cast doubt on the evidence for Plato's biography - Julia Annas has recently done so in order to make the broader case that contemporary problems of Athenian politics are not relevant to the *Republic* (Annas 1999, ch. 4) - but one should not ignore what is there in the dialogues themselves. Plato establishes the connection with the Thirty in the reader's mind by setting a discussion whose climactic theme is tyranny in the location he does, among the dramatic characters he does. What that connection implies is a separate question. If the *Seventh Letter* is some other reader's attempt to draw out those implications, I can only say that, whoever he was, he was a good reader of the *Republic.*

I have drawn on Gigon 1976, pp. 90-91 in order to place Glaucon's classification of goods in the context of the Platonic corpus. The scholarly debate in which this classification is tested against modern moral theories is the one summarized and developed in Annas 1981, pp. 59-71 and Irwin 1995, pp. 189-91. White 1984 resists the anachronism here by connecting Glaucon's classification not with the classifications of goods in other dialogues but with the concept of causation in the *Phaedo.* I do not think of the interpretation in this chapter as incompatible with White's. Plato may well want the reader to connect the sense in which justice within the soul will cause a person to be happy with the account in the *Phaedo* of how fire is the cause of a thing's being hot. But it is not Glaucon who makes this connection, or anything close to it; his classification of goods and his speech are far more revealing of a gentlemanly ethos than of a Platonic metaphysics. So the reader is invited to make a further connection: to see how the gentlemanly ethos is ripe for take-over by a Platonic metaphysics.

The section entitled 'A real man', together with the section that follows it, considers the lure of a manly ethic for one such as Glaucon. In her study of θυμός in Plato, Angela Hobbs has explored this issue in a wide range of dialogues, although her key figure is Callicles rather than Glaucon or Adeimantus (Hobbs 2000, esp. ch. 5.) In the militarism of the philosopher-king she detects, as do I, a means of giving manliness its due (p. 242, 247). The point is complicated but not disarmed by the fact that many of these philosopher-warriors will be women.

I would like to acknowledge the stimulus of the many conversations I had with David McNeill while thinking about the topics of this chapter, particularly the topic of Glaucon's and Adeimantus' characters and of the complex attitude they take towards the pursuit of honour. A study of the values of θυμός in the *Republic* is a principal feature of the dissertation for the University of Chicago (Committee on Social Thought) that he was writing at the time.

CHAPTER 2

City and Soul: Misunderstandings

1. A fork in the road

Let us return to the metaphor of self-guardianship introduced by Adeimantus at 367a. We saw that his was a counsel of individual, gentlemanly perfection in an imperfect world. He regards the person who can control the inferior elements within himself as uncontaminated by them. In response, Socrates sets out to impart an insight into the politics of the soul. The politics within is politics still; it entails compromise; even the healthy soul is not yet pure.

The principal path by which Socrates will convey this insight, a high road that leads through the *Republic* and around which its argument is constructed, is the analogy between soul and city - the elucidation of justice and injustice in the individual by comparison and point-by-point correspondence with justice and injustice in society. It will be the focus of the chapters that follow.

An analogy between city and soul is in fact already implicit in the metaphor of self-guardianship. When Adeimantus claims that the guardian of himself will keep evil from occurring within his soul, he implies a comparison with the policing or protection of social groups, the context in which the term 'guard' or 'guardian' (φύλαξ) has its primary reference. But this is not the direction in which he takes the comparison. Rather than imagine a well-disciplined society that corresponds to the well-disciplined individual, he imagines a society that would require no discipline at all, because each of its members is sufficiently self-disciplined to dispense with social constraint. In a properly educated society, he imagines,

> We would not now be keeping an eye on one another, to guard against injustice. Each man would be keeping an eye on himself. (367a)

This is Adeimantus' version of how a society made up of none but the good would behave - what Socrates in Book 1 hypothesized would be a society in which people would vie with each other *not* to rule (347d). In both cases, uniform excellence among the citizens makes the task of government less urgent.

But we saw in the last chapter that the society Socrates imagines in response to the brothers' challenge does not consist entirely of the good, but is a society in which superior govern inferior. Callipolis is the best society possible for human beings, and as such it is an ideal tempered by realism. Just as Socrates refuses to portray in Callipolis a mere land of Cockaigne, in which potters recline on banqueting couches and take up their wheels when the mood strikes them (420e-421a), so he will not permit Adeimantus to retreat into his quietist - indeed, anarchist - fantasy of uniform self-discipline. Socrates will take the analogy in the direction Adeimantus avoids; he will describe the correspondence between a society and an individual in both of which the superior element is guardian of the inferior. It will be a description tinged with realism, and thereby with regret.

There is a moment in Book 4 (430d) when Socrates' regret comes to the surface. He has described the city's wisdom and its courage and it is time to describe its self-discipline (σωφροσύνη), but he attempts to evade the task, wondering aloud whether there is some way to discover the city's justice without having to bother about its self-discipline. Glaucon has to dissuade him; indeed, it is in order to accommodate Glaucon, it would seem, that Socrates agrees to look into the city's self-discipline after all (430e).

It is a strange moment, the more so since Socrates' declared intention to discover justice as what remains when the other three cardinal virtues have been considered should constrain him not to skip any (428a). Yet it makes sense if we consider that self-discipline is the only one of the city's virtues that requires the city to contain better and worse elements, it being a condition in which better rules worse (οὗ τὸ ἄμεινον τοῦ χείρονος ἄρχει, 431b). It requires Socrates to admit an inferior element into his best city. This bothers Socrates, even if he deems the situation necessary; but it does not bother Glaucon, despite the fact that Socrates elucidates self-discipline in the city by comparing self-discipline in an individual, who must also, therefore, harbor an inferior element within himself (431a). (Notice that only in this one case does Socrates insert an anticipatory account of the corresponding virtue of the individual into his account of the virtue in the city.)

It does not bother him, because like his brother he thinks of individual self-discipline as something completely good, so that even if it entails that there should be a worse part within oneself in need of control, still the exercise of that control makes one superior, and worthy of ruling the inferior elements in the city (431c) - whether or not that worth is appreciated in one's own city.

It is worth retracing to their origin the conditions under which we find Socrates in Book 4 drawing parallels between a city and a soul in which the better element rules the worse. For it turns out to have been an earlier intervention by Glaucon that provided the opportunity. And to grasp this fact is to understand that the situation could have been otherwise.

At the point in Book 2 where Socrates first paused and seemed prepared to think the imaginary city he was constructing might be complete (371e), that 'city' was a small community of farmers and artisans, living in rustic simplicity, having no rulers but the authority of parents and of religion, and cooperating with each other for mutual benefit. Adeimantus is asked whether he can discern the justice and the injustice in such a system. He can only suggest that it resides in some sort of need that the representatives of the various activities in the community have for each other. Socrates says he might be right, and goes on to describe their communal life of rustic contentment.

Here Glaucon intervenes to complain that this life is uncivilized, fit only for a city of pigs (372c-d). His complaint causes Socrates to abandon the account of what he calls 'the genuine and, as it were, healthy version of a city' (ἀληθινὴ πόλις... ὥσπερ ὑγιής τις, 372e) in favour of an examination of the 'swollen and inflamed' city (φλεγμαίνουσα) - the modern city with its luxuries, its need to take from its neighbours, and therefore, crucially, with its warriors, war-leaders, and guardians.

Glaucon's complaint disrupts what might have been a far simpler correspondence between society and individual than the one Socrates eventually develops, had the discussion kept within the ambit of the rudimentary but healthy city. Recall why Socrates had turned to the task of constructing an imaginary community in the first place: in the hope that justice would be easier to discern on the larger scale of a city than in the individual, and that having found it there, we could consider how the just individual - who is the focus of Glaucon's and Adeimantus' interest - resembles the just community in point of justice (369a).

Nothing in this statement of method requires that Socrates apply the correspondence in the manner in which he eventually chooses to apply it, namely as an analogy of elements and structure, according to which the virtues of both the city and the individual are analogous insofar as similar parts of each stand in a similar internal relation to each other and to the whole. Socrates could have followed up Adeimantus' suggestion by finding the justice of his rustic community to consist in the efficiently cooperative manner in which each group provides for the needs of the collective, and then, rather than proceed to consider the individual as a collection of needs and ask how those needs can achieve mutual satisfaction, he could have simply described the just individual as one who makes the appropriate contribution to the collective. That would have been a quite sufficient point of resemblance: the city is called just when it is so organized as to provide for the needs of its citizens; the individual is called just when he cooperates in providing for the needs of his fellow citizens. To be just, on this account, would be to acknowledge the needs of all.

Rather than limit himself to a point of resemblance Socrates works out a correspondence between city and soul that is in effect a proportion. The form of his inquiry is not, as it first appeared: not only X (a person) but also Y (society) can be described as Z (just), so let us look more closely at what X and Y have in common. Rather it becomes: A:B::C:D, where A and B are elements of the society and C and D are elements of the person's soul, and what we must examine, if we wish to discover justice, is the proportion itself. What is more, the relation in which A stands to B in the society and C stands to D in the soul will turn out to be hierarchical. Socrates moves on to consider a city that is no longer a collective, no longer a collection of cooperative individuals, but a hierarchical structure in which some are rulers and others are ruled.

The guardians are introduced by appeal to the principle of 'one man one job' that operated in the collective (374a-e); thus they need only have been fighters for the city in the sense in which the farmers were farming for the city or the builders building for it. Instead, they are given an education in patriotism that causes them to identify their interests not with those of their fellow citizens but with those of the city as a whole, and from their ranks come rulers whose activity takes the whole city as its object, both in itself and in its relations with other cities (428d). And it is quite natural that, in looking for the individual analogue to a city of this type, our thoughts should turn to the internal structure of the individual; for hierarchy of function makes structure stand out in a way that mere multiplicity of function does not.

It is quite natural, but it was not at all inevitable. The fact that a society is hierarchical does not entail that its correspondence to the individual will consist in a proportion. If the city is just because each of its parts, superior and inferior, is acting appropriately, then the individual could be declared just, not because each part of his soul is acting appropriately, but because he, a superior or inferior part of the city, is acting appropriately - is doing his part for the city. Justice is doing one's part, and a just city is so constructed that each person in it does his part.

When the moment arrives for Socrates to steer the city-soul correspondence away from so simple a resolution and towards the complexity of a proportion, Plato's phrasing is cautious. The city's justice has turned out to be a matter of each part, each of its three classes, performing its function, so

> In that case, my friend, if the individual too has these same elements in his soul, we shall feel entitled to expect that it is because these elements are in the same condition in him as they were in the city that he is properly titled by the same names we gave the city. (435b-c)

And Glaucon's response? 'That is quite inevitable' (πᾶσα ἀνάγκη). Yes, it is quite inevitable that, if we go looking for these same elements in the individual soul, and if we find them there, we shall be justified in drawing a proportional analogy between city and soul. But it is not in the least inevitable that we should go looking for these elements in the first place.

The proportional correspondence between city and soul is something Plato writes into the *Republic,* and he tries to ensure we see him writing it in. Because he brings it off by employing suggestions, interruptions, and diversions from the brothers' side, and cautious phrasing on Socrates' side -because he does it this way rather than having Socrates develop a straightforward and committed argument - he is in effect saying to us: 'Be careful, now, with this city-soul analogy of mine. Don't swallow it whole. Certainly you should examine it on its merits; but do not *simply* examine it on its merits. Ask yourself why I chose to introduce it without justification. I chose to introduce it; I had my reasons; but I did not tell you my reasons. So think about what they were.'

That the analogy between city and soul is an analogy of elements and structure has far-reaching consequences for any conclusions one might

41

draw about Plato's purposes in the *Republic*. In order to explain those consequences, I will turn first to two important ways in which the analogy has been misunderstood, in the interpretations of Bernard Williams and of Jonathan Lear.[5]

2. Williams' challenge

Williams makes problems for the analogy out of two claims to which he believes Socrates appeals in establishing it:

> [1] A city is F if and only if its people are F (435e).
> [2] The explanation of a city's being F is the same as that of a person's being F (435a).

Following these principles through in the case of justice, Williams points out that if a city's justice is to be explained in the same way as an individual's justice, the city will be just because each of its three elements - thoughtful, spirited, and materialistic or appetitive - is doing its respective job. But the rule that a city is F only if its people are F will apply equally to the city's elements, which consist, after all, of people; that is, an element of the city will be spirited only if the people that constitute it are spirited, and so on. But then the just city will consist of three classes: thoughtful people, spirited people, appetitive people, with the last group, as the *Republic* makes clear, being much the largest. But an appetitive person can hardly be a just person. So the just city will not after all consist of just people, as rule 1 says it must.

Williams extracts this rule from the passage in which Socrates appeals to stereotypical ethnic characteristics - the Thracians' and Scythians' reputation for spiritedness, the Athenians' for love of learning, the Phoenicians' and Egyptians' for the commercial instinct - in order to show that such characteristics must first be present in the people before they can be present in the community (435e). And Williams is quite right to find the rule at least suggested here. It is in the nature of an ethnic stereotype to be applied with a broad brush: all Athenians are cultured, all Thracians are warlike, all Semites are mercenary, all Cretans are liars, and so on. That is why these examples at least superficially justify the claim that there are *in each*

---

5 Williams 1973; Lear 1992.

of us the same characteristics as in the city; for we are imagining communities that have, quite implausibly, only one ethnic characteristic - the characteristic exemplified by all of their members.

Rather than seize on this rule and turn it to paradox, as Williams does, I will begin with the fact that the rule would lead to paradox, and ask what Plato therefore intended by suggesting that rule. Within the fiction, all Socrates need be doing here is giving a *prima facie* reason to expect characteristics at the level of the city to reappear at the level of the individual, on the grounds, as he says, that they could not have found their way into the city from any other source. Socrates begins by making his position seem plausible and familiar to his audience. But what Plato is doing is to allow the reader to see how very different from this is Socrates' eventual procedure, and how different are the results he obtains, when comparing the just city to the just individual.

For the just city is not presented as monolithic, unlike Athens, Thrace, or Egypt, but as divided into three classes of sharply divergent character. Indeed, it would be tempting to think of it as a city of Athenian rulers, Thracian soldiers, and Egyptian artisans and farmers. In other words, it is hard to resist asking, as Williams asks: Surely the individual ruler in the just city will have a soul led by its thoughtful part? Surely the individual soldier must have a soul led by its spirited part? And will the individual artisan or farmer not have a soul led by its appetitive part? But as it turns out, the analogy gives no answers to these questions.

By the principle that the individual's justice is to be explained in the same way as the city's justice (435b; compare Williams' second rule), the individual will have within him elements equivalent to these three classes in the city, and related in the same way. What makes the city wise is a particular class within it; what makes the individual wise is an equivalent element in his character. What makes the city just is a relation among its classes; what makes the individual just is an equivalent relation between equivalent elements of his character.

Nothing in the operation of this analogy dictates that the wise or just individual should be a member of any of the classes in the wise or just city. Spirited Thracians must be present in spirited Thrace, because when we say that Thrace is spirited, we really only mean to say that Thracians are. In this case, Williams' first rule holds. But this is not how the analogy between city and soul operates. The fact that an individual has a character constructed analogously to a certain kind of city does not entail that he should be a member of it; likewise, the analogy has nothing to say about whether the virtues of the virtuous individual are to be found in the members of any class within the virtuous city.

This is especially clear in the two instances described in Book 4 where a virtue of the city is monopolized by a single class within the city - that is, in the case of wisdom and courage - because these are the cases where we might be most inclined to assume that the wise class is made up of wise individuals, the courageous class made up of courageous ones. But consider: The wisdom of a ruling guardian is knowledge of what is good for his city, statesmanship (428d), the wisdom of the virtuous individual - a wisdom limited by the context of Book 4 to practical reason - is knowledge of what is good for himself (442c). But anyone who reads newspapers can see that it is quite possible for a good statesman not to know what is good for himself. The courage of a soldier-guardian is the courage to face dangers to the city, and is inculcated in him by the rulers (429c-430c); but the courage of the virtuous individual is the ability to face down fears of whatever kind, as instructed by his own powers of reason (442b-c). At 430c Socrates emphasises the fact that the courage of the soldier-guardian is courage of a particular kind, courage 'as it relates to the city' (πολιτικήν γε).

This is not, of course, to rule out that the statesman in the just city could also be a wise individual, could also know what is good for himself. It is simply to say that the analogy neither rules it out nor rules it in. If the statesman also happens to be a wise individual, this would come about because of regularities in human nature - for example, the tendency of good statesmen to be thoughtful people, and of thoughtful people to know what is good for themselves. If true, it would not be by virtue of the analogy between city and soul that it is true.

Although the operation of the analogy is clearest in these two instances, it is no different when we come to those virtues of the city which are not restricted to a single class: the city's self-discipline and its justice.

If we are inclined to assume that the wise class is made up of wise individuals, we might also assume that the just city is made up of just individuals. Certainly, each person in the just city performs his own task (τὸ αὑτοῦ ἕκαστος εἷς ὢν ἔπραττε, 433d); but this is not to say that each is a just individual. As the just city is one in which each element performs its proper task, so too with the just individual (441d-e). But the elements of the just individual are the parts of his soul; he is the person in whom reason, spirit, and appetite perform their proper tasks; and this is not at all what it means for an individual in the just city to perform *his* proper task. That task is simply the job that society requires of him and to which his abilities fit him. One man will make a good potter, another a good soldier, yet another a good ruler. If each does what he is fit to do and in particular does not attempt to do a job that is the prerogative of a different class (434b), the city is just, and its analogy with the just individual is complete. That analogy does not peer into the souls of the individuals who make up the just city, but only into the soul of the individual to whom the just city is analogous.

This is not to rule out that a member of the just city could be a just individual, any more than a statesman in the just city is excluded from being a wise individual. If the analogy does not peer into the souls of the members of the just city, we are free to do so ourselves, and ask, for example, whether a craftsman in that city would need to have a soul ruled by reason - the soul of a just individual - if he is to be willing to keep his humble station without resentment. To that particular question Socrates will imply a negative answer in Book 9: a manual worker lacks strength in the best part of his soul; his reasoning part is too weak to rule his soul, to govern his life; therefore, if he is to be so far as possible under the same kind of rule as the best person, his soul should be ruled by that best person, which is to say by one whose soul is ruled by its reasoning part (590c-d). The manual worker is a natural follower, not a natural leader. But this conclusion is not deduced from the analogy between city and soul. It is not a resemblance between the manual worker's soul and a certain type of city that licenses Socrates to draw his conclusions. What lies behind them is a social attitude, the disdain felt towards those who work with their hands or engage in menial tasks, a disdain that Socrates justifies by appeal to the condition of their souls.

The account of self-discipline in the city is exceptional in that it begins with a discussion of the individual - with an analysis of individual self-mastery. As a result it is harder to discern that even in this instance no implications are drawn from the analogy about the presence or absence of self-disciplined individuals within the self-disciplined city.

Socrates claims that the city's self-discipline resembles a musical harmony (430e), and points to what people say about the virtue of self-discipline in general: it is a kind of 'order' (κόσμος); it is 'a mastery of pleasures and desires' (ἡδονῶν τινων καὶ ἐπιθυμιῶν ἐγκράτεια); and this mastery is also expressed as 'being master of oneself' (κρείττω αὑτοῦ). Analysis of the concept of self-mastery in an individual shows that it amounts to the mastery of what is better in a man's soul over what is worse, the worse part being larger and more various than the better. The analogue in the ideal city is not far to seek. There too, the superior element - the guardian minority - is in charge of the inferior element - the mass of farmers and artisans (431a-b).

But self-mastery was in particular the mastery of pleasures and desires. What is the analogue for this in a city? It is that among the masses one tends to find 'the whole range and variety of desires, pleasures, and pains' (πολλὰς καὶ παντοδαπὰς ἐπιθυμίας καὶ ἡδονὰς καὶ λύπας), whereas 'simple, moderate desires, which are guided by rational calculation, using intelligence and correct belief' (τὰς δέ γε ἁπλᾶς τε καὶ μετρίας, αἳ δὴ μετὰ νοῦ τε καὶ δόξης ὀρθῆς λογισμῷ ἄγονται) tend to be found among the best born and best educated (431c). This is certainly so in Callipolis; and since the desires found among the masses are there controlled 'by the desires and the wisdom' (ὑπό τε τῶν ἐπιθυμιῶν καὶ τῆς φρονήσεως) found among their superiors, the guardians, the city can be called not only master of itself, but also master of its pleasures and desires (κρείττω ἡδονῶν τε καὶ ἐπιθυμιῶν) (431d).

If it is important to understand that the analogy does not make the self-discipline of the city conditional on the self-discipline of its members, it is equally important to understand that Socrates is not making it his project here to declare the general populace of Callipolis lacking in the individual self-discipline that the guardians possess. The general populace of Callipolis are given no special education; their lives are built around their families and the provision of material goods; their personal values and priorities cannot be expected to differ much from those ascribed to peasants and manual workers anywhere. They will take their pleasures at the table and between the sheets; they will be proud of their children and promote their children's interests over those of others' children; they will envy and quarrel with their immediate neighbours.

By contrast with the dignified pleasures thought appropriate to the best-bred and best-educated, their earthy, colourful behaviour can be said to represent or correspond to the multifarious appetites that are controlled in the self-disciplined individual. And this is how Callipolis, in which an austere and well-educated guardian class is in control of the farmers and artisans, can be described as 'master of its pleasures and desires'.

But this is not to say that the farmers and artisans of Callipolis will lack self-discipline as individuals; nor, indeed, to deny it. Socrates expects Glaucon to be able to see, on the basis of the civic arrangements already described ('do you see these same qualities in your city?', οὐκοῦν καὶ ταῦτα ὁρᾷς ἐνόντα σοι ἐν τῇ πόλει, 431c), that in Callipolis the desires of the masses are controlled by their rulers. But the only way in which we have seen guardians controlling these desires is by actions at the level of public policy, not by surveillance of individual decency. We have heard that they must maintain both a ceiling and a floor for the income of craftsmen, and must ensure that the city does not grow too large (421c-422a, 423b-c, 434b). They will also maintain restrictions on public entertainment (398a-b). But in Callipolis - that is, in what has been said or implied about Callipolis - there are no protectors of public virtue whipping women in the streets for revealing an ankle; no resident informers reporting on their neighbours in each state-owned block of apartments.

Socrates is not speaking of the behaviour of individuals; he is speaking of the pleasures and tastes of whole classes. Rather than describe the appetites *of* the masses or *of* the well-bred, he describes the appetites *found among* the masses, *found among* the well-bred, using the preposition ἐν throughout. Self-discipline in the individual is presented as the control of an inferior and multifarious part of the person by a smaller, superior part (431a). It is not presented as the control of desire by reason. So the analogue at the level of the city will not be, say, the control of a pleasure-loving class by a class of rational men, but the control of a class whose pleasures and desires are multifarious by a class whose pleasures and desires are simple and measured.

The pleasures and priorities of such a city considered as a whole will reflect those of its ruling class - hence Callipolis will stay small, maintain decorum in its public entertainment, banish luxuries from the economy even as it permits elegance in public art and architecture (401b). The public life of Callipolis is the context that Socrates evokes in his discussion of the city's self-discipline. The individual self-discipline of cobblers and carpenters forms no part of Socrates' context. So the passage offers no target for the objection Williams aims at those who think powerful and disorderly desires endemic to cobblers and carpenters.[6]

For similar reasons, Socrates' confidence that in this above all other cities there will be agreement among rulers and ruled about which of them is to rule (431d-e) ought not to puzzle us. It makes excellent sense, provided we do not suppose that the farmers and artisans are here presented as a mass of individuals in each of whom powerful appetites and resentments brew. The farmer and artisan class of Callipolis is materialistic and practical. It is well suited, then, to appreciate the rule of impartial and incorruptible officials who do not enrich themselves at the expense of the citizenry, who impose minimal taxes, maintain a stable economy, prevent the neighbour who might flaunt his wealth from becoming wealthy in the first place, promote public piety and order, and take upon themselves the entire military burden of defending their citizens' farms and families.

Nor, finally, is it puzzling to conclude that self-discipline is not confined to any particular class in the city but is 'to be found in' (ἐνεῖναι) both the rulers and the ruled, and that this is what it means to say the city's self-discipline resembles a musical harmony (431e). There is no suggestion here that a city is self-disciplined only if its citizens are, or even that a city is self-disciplined only if its different classes of citizen are. It is a mistake to wonder how self-discipline applies to each class: to suppose, as Williams or Annas do, that the members of the lowest class exhibit self-discipline by doffing the cap to their betters, provided their powerful appetites do not paralyse the gesture; or to suppose, as Vegetti does, that the ruling class exhibits self-discipline by remaining guard-dogs and not permitting themselves to become wolves.[7] It is the city as a whole that exhibits self-discipline, in its harmony of different interests and abilities - in the consensual balance between its wise government, powerful army, and productive masses (432a).

[6] Williams 1973, 204.
[7] Williams 1973, 204, Annas 1981, 115-17, Vegetti, ed. 1998 [vol. 3], 25.

We can safely conclude that Williams' rule 1, the rule that a city is F if and only if its citizens are F, does not underlie the city-soul analogy. But neither does a diluted form of it, the idea that

[3] A city is F if and only if its leading, most influential, or predominant citizens are F.

Readers of Book 8 may find it very natural to think that the timocratic city is the city ruled by the class of timocratic individuals, that an oligarchy is ruled by oligarchic characters, and so on. But Williams shows that paradox results from the application of this rule also.

Most obviously, when we come to the account of democracy and of the democratic man, we find that the individual is a person of labile character, shifting readily among many preferences of life-style. In this he corresponds to the democratic society, which contains within itself all manner of characters, and permits many different styles of life. But the predominant class in a democracy is the populace, and by our new rule, that populace will have the character of the democratic man; so the majority in a democratic city will have the same character, the labile character of the democratic man. But how can this be reconciled with the description of democracy as containing all manner of characters?

Once again the principle that leads to paradox seems to be suggested by a remark that Socrates makes. To justify the idea that for each type of unsound regime there exists a correspondingly unsound character-type, he points out that regimes do not spring from nowhere, but arise from the characters of a city's inhabitants, the ones which tip the scales and draw the rest of the city with them (544e). And once again, as with the Thracians and Phoenicians, the appeal to how societies come to be as they are does not properly support the operation of the analogy as Socrates actually applies it.

I should first point out that I have just translated the sentence at 544e in a way which favours Williams' interpretation of it. But so far as the Greek goes, the claim may be no more than a repetition of the point about Thrace and the Thracians enunciated at 435e, rather than a development of it. That is, the clause ἃ ἂν ὥσπερ ῥέψαντα τἆλλα ἐφελκύσηται, 'which tip the scale, as it were, taking the rest with them', would express the generalization that individual characters in a city outweigh every other factor when it comes to determining the overall character of the city. The word τἆλλα would not refer to other individual characters but to factors other than individual character.

But to return to the sentence as Williams understands it: This time we have, not ethnic stereotypes, but a platitude about political change. Those who take control of a society get to stamp the whole society with the particular values of their group - be they aristocratic, oligarchic, or democratic. The Greek world offered plenty of examples of such changes of regime. Whenever we encounter a particular type of regime, then, we have a *prima facie* reason to look for a type of person who was its moving force, and imposed his values upon it.

We have already seen that the wisdom of the ruler in the virtuous society is quite different from the wisdom of the correspondingly virtuous individual, and this by itself would show that the predominance rule does not describe the workings of the city-soul analogy any better than its predecessor. That is, the city is wise, but not because the predominant individuals within it are wise; for those individuals, the rulers, are not wise in the same sense in which individuals are wise. They represent the city's wisdom as a class; but this will not give us the result we seek, if we are looking to find timocratic individuals in power in a timocracy, democratic individuals in power in a democracy, and so on. Close scrutiny of the way in which Socrates applies the analogy in the case of the unsound types of society and of persons reveals that, so far as the analogy goes, there is no more justification for locating those men and their vices among the ruling classes of the corresponding cities than we earlier found to locate the virtuous man among the members of the virtuous city.

3. Lear's dilemma

In subsequent chapters I will give those passages of Books 8 and 9 the detailed examination they require; but for now let us consider the apparent predicament in which we are left once we have decided that Williams' paradoxes do not in fact have any grip on the operation of the city-soul analogy.

Although we have evaded Williams' unpalatable conclusions, we have also radically disengaged the soul from the city. Natural curiosity about people's lives in the various societies described, and about the place in those societies of the corresponding individuals, has been blocked. The descriptions of the various societies and the corresponding individuals run on parallel but entirely separate tracks. And so we might well ask: Is there any point to this duplication? Individuals live in societies and both shape and are shaped by them; in which case, even if we agree that separate consideration of societies and individuals makes for a clearer account of their respective virtues and vices than would have been possible had their interactions been described, still, we surely have a right to expect the two terms of the analogy to be joined, when the analogy is done, by a connection less weak than mere analogical correspondence. Otherwise society and individual may seem simply to have fallen apart. And that would be the last thing we want to find in a work that purports to deal with justice.

This is the predicament in which Jonathan Lear finds himself, and his response is to restore to the analogy the causal-psychological relations that it seems to mask. Those relations would be of two kinds, both omnipresent, according to Lear, in the *Republic*: internalization and externalization.

Internalization is the process by which society fashions the individual for the role he is to play in it - normally, by education and by the influence of those social groups with which he comes in contact while his character is still developing. Externalization is the pay-back: the socially formed individual does his part to mould the society around him and educate the next generation along the lines of the precepts and preferences that he has internalized. These causal relations between society and individual are the ground on which the purely formal relations of the analogy stand - the formal relations that Williams expressed in the principles that we have seen lead to paradox.

Lear rejects Williams' first rule, that a city is F if and only if its men are; but externalization is, in effect, Lear's causal version of Williams' rule 3, the predominance rule. Thus, speaking of our familiar passage about the Thracians and Phoenicians, he says:

> Plato believes the formal relation holds in virtue of causal-psychological transactions. Plato's point (at 435e) is not that a spirited polis, say, is spirited simply in virtue of having spirited citizens,

> but in having spirited citizens who are successful in shaping the polis in their image.[8]

In other words, a city is F only if its predominant citizens are F; and the mode of their predominance is specified as successful externalization.

Internalization and externalization would turn the city-soul analogy into an epiphenomenon of deeper causal relations, and make the parallel tracks of society and individual converge. But while it is undeniable that internalization is important to the *Republic* - in the sense that the work makes much of the influence of culture on the individual, both for good and for bad, and gives education a central place among social institutions - internalization is never invoked in order to ground the city-soul analogy. Timocratic, oligarchic, democratic, and tyrannical individuals do not get to be that way by virtue of having internalized the culture of timocracies, oligarchies, democracies, and tyrannies. We are certainly given an account of how their characters are formed, how they are corrupted by forces at work in their family and in their environment, but no connection is made thereby to the cities to which they correspond. Rather, the account runs once again in parallel to a quite separate account of how the corresponding city was formed - an account that is causally independent of the individual's development, although analogous to it. Despite our best efforts, the text does not permit us to break through the barrier of the parallelism to a direct causal-psychological connnection with the corresponding societies.

Externalization plays no more part in grounding the city-soul analogy than does internalization. Timocratic, oligarchic, and democratic societies are not ruled by timocratic, oligarchic, and democratic individuals who have succeeded in moulding their societies in their own image. When it comes to Callipolis, however, Lear thinks that the text describes just such an act of externalization, in its account of how the philosopher-king - who as a philosophic individual is analogous to Callipolis - has within his soul a clear 'pattern' or 'model', a παράδειγμα, which he has acquired through his knowledge of eternal realities (484c); how his contemplation of these realities has brought him to resemble and imitate them (500c); and how, like a painter, he paints his image of justice on the canvas of Callipolis by

---

[8] Lear 1992, 195.

looking to the reality of justice among the eternal forms (484d). These passages appear to describe the philosopher externalizing a pattern that he has first internalized; this would be how Callipolis and the soul of the philosopher-king come to be structured alike.

In chapter 4 we will come back to the question of the philosopher-king's relation to Callipolis, and see then what truth there is in Lear's claim. We will look too at the relation between the tyrannical individual and a tyranny, and discover that it is here, not in the philosopher's relation to Callipolis, that externalization is truly at work; also, that its work here is the exception, not the rule. But first we must learn to embrace the fact that the city-soul correspondence is indeed an analogy, nothing more, nothing less. We must examine the mechanism of that analogy at its most complex, in the parallel descriptions of unsound societies and individuals. It will help to begin by probing its origins, and by considering what kind of analogy it is.

Sources and Scholarly Contexts for Chapter 2

The interpretation of the city-soul analogy that will emerge in the chapters still to come shows up with particular clarity when set against the forceful and explicit arguments of Williams and of Lear, and that is one reason for making them the focus here. But equally important is that Williams' arguments in particular have had a strong influence over others. Indeed, it is precisely because Lear thinks Williams' the most penetrating critique of Plato's analogy we have that he sets out to modify the principles it attributes to Plato (Lear 1992, p. 194). Nor is he alone. Many prominent scholars continue to think of the problems isolated by Williams as genuine problems for Plato's account, and many continue to hold the false assumptions about how the city-soul analogy works that generated those problems in the first place.

Annas 1981, for example, which is still the standard introduction to the *Republic* for English-speaking students, enshrines and endorses in its chapter 'Parts and virtues of state and soul' the basic problems that Williams poses (see pp. 146-51). Annas uses the analogy to peer into the souls of individual members of the just city ('desire being the part that is dominant in the souls of the members of the productive class', p. 149). And she treats the problem Williams makes for the correspondence between democracy and the democratic man- a problem that depends on the predominance rule - as the final and complete breakdown of an analogy that was always in trouble (p. 302).

There are three connected errors at work in the most recent scholarly literature, and they are to be found across several scholarly cultures. One is endorsing the predominance rule; the other, using the analogy to peer into the souls of members of the city to which a type of individual corresponds; and the last, which is Lear's error, is refusing to accept that the analogy is just an analogy, insisting instead that it also links city and soul by causal relations. For example, Otfried Höffe's chapter on the city-soul analogy in Höffe ed., 1997 endorses the predominance rule while attempting to evade the 'Williamsschen Aporien' (p. 92). Similarly, Höffe continues to give the analogy a causal twist even as he distinguishes his position from Lear's ('Auf diese weise besteht zwischen dem Politischen und dem Psychologischen nicht bloss eine Analogie, sondern sogar eine Interdependenz', p. 78). Dorothea Frede's chapter on the unsound societies and individuals in the same volume assumes that oligarchic individuals rule in oligarchies (p. 260), democratic individuals in democracies (p. 263), and generalizes the predominance rule thus: 'Platons Analyse der Entstehung der Repräsentanten der einzelnen Staatsformen immer auf die Mitglieder der *Oberklasse* beschränkt' (p. 267). The same assumption is made by Reeve 1988, p. 261.

Mario Vegetti attempts to mitigate rather than dispell problems posed originally by Williams, and in the process shows that he considers Plato's account vulnerable to some at least of them, even if not all (Vegetti ed., 1998 [vol. 3], p. 26, 42; contrast p. 39). He assumes that the analogy licenses structural claims about the souls of the members of the different classes in Callipolis (pp. 41-43); he endorses the predominance rule (p. 27); and he adds a causal dimension to the isomorphism, in words that recall the reciprocity of internalization and externalization in Lear: 'Questa forma di giustizia [viz. justice within the tripartite soul] connette l'anima alla città in un nesso che non è soltanto isomorfico, ma di reciproca implicazione causale. Tanto più infatti la città potrà essere giusta quanto più lo saranno le anime dei suoi cittadini... reciprocamente, la giustizia nell'anima è l'esito dell'impresa educativa globale della città...' (p. 40).

Some scholars, certainly, have avoided these errors, both before and since Williams wrote. A notable example is Irwin 1995, p. 230: 'When [Plato] claims that the structure of the virtuous soul corresponds to that of the ideal city, he implies only that it must have the same parts in the same relation; he does not imply that individuals in a city that has a given virtue must also have that virtue'. Blössner 1997, p. 179, with nn. 492, 493, traces this feature of the scholarship over a long period (compare Irwin 1995, p. 383 n. 9). One can only say, however, that it has never become a dominant trend.

It is Williams' article that Gail Fine chooses to reprint in a collection intended to define Platonic studies for the next generation of graduate students (Fine ed., 1999). This article endures in part by virtue of its undoubted philosophic brilliance and by the exquisiteness of its puzzles. But another factor contributing to its influence has been the greater interest of scholars in the psychology of the various individuals described by the analogy than in the civic life of the corresponding cities. Irwin, for example, having sidestepped Williams' problems, has nothing further to say about the workings of the analogy. His chapter on Books 8-9 (Irwin 1995, pp. 281-97) focusses exclusively on the inner workings of the souls of the unjust individuals. A similar focus on the individual soul is to be found in such important contributions as those of Cooper 1984, Kahn 1987, or Gill 1996, ch. 4. The effect is to leave Williams' interpretation free to set the agenda of those who wish to examine the analogy itself.

My approach in this chapter has been to defuse Williams' problems directly. A different approach would be to accept the problems as valid but assume that Plato created them deliberately. This is what Norbert Blössner does, incorporating Williams' arguments into his own in order to demonstrate that Plato did not intend the analogy to hold in an objectively valid way, but instead employs it as a literary tool directed at a larger argument (Blössner 1997, pp. 164-65 with n. 453). Blössner does not, however, incorporate Williams' arguments whole. His awareness of how hard it is to apply the predominance rule in every instance, for example, is admirable. But he concludes (p. 181 n. 493): '... die Beziehung zwischen den Menschen *in* der Polis und den Menschen als *Analoga* der Polis notorisch unklar bleibt. Für jede Ordnung scheint die Frage anders zu beantworten. Eine einheitliche und konsequente Lösung dürfte kaum zu finden sein; offensichtlich war die Herstellung eines konsistenten Schemas nicht Platons anliegen.'

In what follows I will uncover a pattern in the analogy which, if it is not 'einheitlich', is nevertheless 'konsistent'. Blössner's account will come up repeatedly, since its combination of thoroughness and insight puts it in a class apart from all other investigations of the city-soul analogy. I have found several of my own points anticipated in Blössner's book. He notes, for example, as I do in this chapter, that there is no inevitability about how the analogy develops into a proportional likeness (p. 156), and that self-rule and the ability to rule a city need not go hand in hand (p. 160 n. 442). Ultimately, to be sure, our accounts are quite different. But that is something for later chapters to show.

CHAPTER 3

City and Soul: A Metaphorical Understanding

1. A proportional metaphor

The correspondences between the several varieties of society and soul considered in the *Republic* depend on similarities between the two domains, the social and the individual. Does this make those correspondences an elaborate species of metaphor, or simile? Certainly, the work is not short of extended similes, which it designates by the appropriate Greek term εἰκών: notably when political life is compared to life on board a ship (487e), when the soul is compared to a multiform, mythical beast (588b); and when education and enlightenment is compared to emergence from a cave (514a, 517a). There is also the complex comparison between the sophist and an animal-handler at 493a-c, which is not called an εἰκών, but is introduced by the phrase 'it is as if...' (οἷόνπερ ἂν εἰ).

But the parallelism between city and soul should not be classed among these similes. In their case, it is perfectly clear which of the elements is the target of comparison. We are not interested in a tour of the cave as spelunkers but only in what its prisoners and parapet and statues and the cave itself correspond to, that is, in what Socrates is using them to say about that target domain.

Not so with city and soul. Although the parallelism is formally introduced for the purpose of discovering what justice is in the individual - that is, by looking for it first in the context of the city, where it will be easier to see (368d-e) - and the target of comparison might appear as a result to be the individual rather than the city, it is very, very difficult to believe that political institutions and reforms so intricately developed as those of Callipolis appear in the *Republic* for no other reason than comparison with the inner mechanism of the virtuous soul. Gauging the balance of Plato's interest between city and soul, between politics and morality, has always been a problem for readers of this work. If we think of the city-soul analogy as a simile, then, it would be one in which the comparison could swing in either direction.

In fact the various parallel analyses of cities and of souls are never called similes, εἰκόνες, nor are they introduced in the manner of similes. The relation between the two domains is described as similarity or as correspondence; that is all. Here are some of those descriptions: 'Now let us apply our findings to the individual, and if they agree...' (ἐπαναφέρωμεν εἰς τὸν ἕνα, κἂν μὲν ὁμολογῆται... 434e); the individual 'will be like the just city' (ὅμοιος ἔσται, 435b); 'the man who corresponds to this regime' (ὁ κατὰ ταύτην τὴν πολιτείαν ἀνήρ, 548d); 'the man who resembles it' (τὸν δὲ ταύτῃ ὅμοιον, 553a); 'let us consider who someone of this type is as an individual' (τίς ὁ τοιοῦτος ἰδίᾳ, 558c); 'the man of tyrannical character remains to be considered' (λοιπὸς... ὁ τυραννικὸς ἀνήρ, 571a); 'the similarity between the city and the man' (τὴν ὁμοιότητα... τῆς τε πόλεως καὶ τοῦ ἀνδρός, 577c); 'if, then, the man is similar to the city' (εἰ οὖν ὅμοιος ἀνὴρ τῇ πόλει, 577d).

But this is not to say that the correspondence between city and soul is anything other than analogical. It certainly might have been, as we saw in the previous chapter. The justice of the larger thing, society, could have amounted to its recognizing the needs of all citizens, and so too could the justice of the smaller thing, the individual. Or the relation between them could have been like that between Thrace and the Thracians, and the city would have been declared virtuous on the grounds that it was made up of virtuous citizens. In either case, the similarity would have been causal, not merely analogical; the virtuous society would have been seen as the causal sum of the relations between its virtuous components, the citizens, or as the causal sum of their characteristics.

Instead, Socrates pursues the causal relations between whole and part on separate tracks. Callipolis is virtuous because of the three classes of citizens it contains and the relations between those classes; the individual is virtuous because of the three elements that make up his soul and the relations between those elements. The relations between the elements of the human soul and the classes of Callipolis, however, are analogical, not causal. Reason is like a wise ruler and guardian, spirit like an honourable soldier and an ally of reason, appetite like a moneymaker and materialist. Socrates elaborates the causal connections between these parts with a wealth of metaphorical detail: spirit follows the 'instructions' (παραγγελθέν) of its 'ruler' (ἄρχων), reason, which has the job of deliberating for the whole 'community' (κοινόν), all of whose members 'are of one opinion' (ὁμοδοξῶσι) as to who should rule, and do not fall into 'civil strife' (στασιάζωσιν) (442b-c). In the account of corrupt characters in Book 8 the level of metaphoric elaboration rises to the rococo. While these civic metaphors cement the parallelism between individual and society, they have nothing to say about the causal connections between the two. Indeed, they only serve to emphasize that the correspondence is analogical rather than causal.

The kernel of the correspondence between city and soul is what Aristotle would call a proportional metaphor or simile (μεταφορὰ κατὰ τὸ ἀνάλογον) - one that implies or states a ratio.[9] Aristotle declares this the most celebrated type of metaphor, and attributes a nice example to Pericles: the city's youth who perished in the war disappeared from the state as if someone had removed the springtime from the year (*Rhetoric* 3.10.7). The metaphor implies a ratio: the city's youth (νεότης) stand to the city as springtime stands to the year. And being a ratio, it is 'convertible' (δεῖ ἀνταποδιδόναι, *Rhetoric* 3.4.4). The youth are the city's springtime, but equally, springtime is the youth of the year. In the later treatise known as 'Demetrius' *On Style* (Περὶ Ἑρμηνείας) this reversibility is illustrated - if somewhat inexactly - with a metaphor more pertinent to our subject:

> There is a resemblance between a general, a helmsman, and a charioteer; they are all in command (πάντες γὰρ οὗτοι ἄρχοντές εἰσιν). So we can safely call a general the helmsman of the state, and conversely call a helmsman the ruler (ἄρχοντα) of the ship. (78)

In the *Republic,* the art of ruling others is already in Book 1 included in a proportional simile, when Thrasymachus asserts that rulers stand to their subjects as to sheep (343b), allowing us to fill in the fourth term by noting his sardonic twist on the famous Homeric metaphor of the king as shepherd of his people. If the king is shepherd of his people, then the shepherd would be king of his sheep. But it is rather with the similarity between the ruler and the doctor than that between ruler and shepherd that the *Republic* runs the metaphor explicitly in both directions, for Socrates in Book 1 calls the doctor a 'ruler over bodies' (σωμάτων ἄρχων, 342d), and in Book 3 (389b), describing how the rulers of Callipolis must administer beneficial lies to the city as a kind of medicine, calls these rulers 'doctors' - that is, doctors of the city.

---

[9] *Poetics* 21 [1457b]; *Rhetoric* 3.4.4 [1407a], 3.10.7 [1411a].

By the time we get to Book 4, then, we are primed for the proportional metaphor from which the city-soul correspondence develops: that reason is the ruler of the soul. For this implies that reason stands to the soul as rulers stand to the city, so that if reason is the ruler of the soul, then rulers are the reason - the wisdom or intelligence - of the city. And when I say that the city-soul correspondence 'develops' from the first of these two metaphors, I do not mean that it is argued on this basis, rather I mean that this metaphor can be regarded as the seed in Plato's mind from which the city-soul analogy came to grow.

It would not have been a metaphor familiar to Plato's audience from their cultural heritage. Certainly, it is not foreign to that heritage to conceive of psychological forces either as being in control of a person or, more rarely, as being in control of other psychological forces. But that control is not depicted as political. The metaphors most frequently encountered are of struggle or battle, of superior strength or power, of mastery; of addressing commands or encouragement; of taking the helm and steering; but not unambiguously of kingship or of government. Had Gorgias meant by λόγος the power of thought or reasoning when he called it a 'mighty potentate' (δυνάστης μέγας) in his *Helen* (8), this would have stood out as an exception (and it remains an interesting precedent in its own way); but in context the word means 'language', not reasoning.

Instead we find Homer's heroes attempting to conquer or master their spirit (θυμός), resisting or succumbing to its prompts and commands, speaking to it in return with words of encouragement or reproof. After Homer we find metaphors in which the controlling element is not the person or his spirit but his mind or his good sense (νόος, φρένες), but still the imagery is of steering or of being superior or stronger, rather than of ruling. Sometimes the possibility implicit in such metaphors that our good sense could lose the struggle is made explicit.

A representative list would include Theognis 630-1: νόος should be but is not always stronger (κρέσσων) than θυμός; Aeschylus *Persae* 767: Medus' son achieved hegemony because 'his intelligence plied the steering-oar of his θυμός', φρένες γὰρ αὐτοῦ θυμὸν ᾠακοστρόφουν; Euripides *Medea* 1021-80: Medea's soliloquy, the classic case of reason being overpowered - parodied in Aristophanes *Acharnians* 480-4; Euripides fr. 718.1 (Nauck): 'it is time for your judgment to be stronger than your θυμός', ὥρα σε θυμοῦ κρείσσονα γνώμην ἔχειν; Heraclitus fr. B85 and Democritus fr. B236

(Diels-Kranz), both beginning 'it is difficult to fight with θυμός', θυμῷ μάχεσθαι χαλεπόν, with Heraclitus continuing, 'whatever it wants, it buys from the soul', and Democritus, 'but conquering it (κρατέειν) is the mark of a man of good sense (εὐλογίστου)'; Democritus fr. B290: 'Cast out by reasoning (λογισμῷ) the ungovernable (ἀδέσποτον) grief of a benumbed soul'. Notice also the Pindaric fragment cited by Cephalus in the *Republic,* 331a, on how hope steers judgment (ἐλπὶς... γνώμαν κυβερνᾷ).

Still less do we find in Plato's cultural heritage anything like the converse of the metaphor that reason is the ruler of the soul, namely that rulers are the wisdom or the intelligence of the city. Poets personify the city freely, of course. The city 'strives' in Pindar (μάρναται, *Nemean* 5.47), 'rejoices' or feels fear in Aristophanes (γέγηθεν, *Knights* 1417; κἂν φόβῳ καθημένη, *Peace* 642), and so on. But there is no pattern of comparison between classes or individuals within the city and any of the personified city's feelings and thoughts, or capacities for feeling and thought. So far as I have been able to discover, not only is there no such pattern of metaphor in Plato's heritage, there is no instance of any such metaphor. But searches with so broad a scope are inherently fallible.

When poets personify the city, however, they do so just as often by giving it a body as by giving it a mind. In the line from the *Knights* just cited, Aristophanes has the city 'go pale' (ὠχριῶσα) as well as feel fear. Theognis' city is 'pregnant' (κυεῖ, 39 West), Solon's has a 'wound' (ἕλκος, 4.17 West), Aeschylus' 'groans aloud' (βοᾷ, *Agamemnon* 1106). While we do not quite find the metaphor of the king as the eye of the city - which could be thought of as the bodily equivalent of the idea that rulers are the intelligence of the city - we do find this: 'the presence of the master I consider the eye of the household (ὄμμα γὰρ δόμων νομίζω δεσπότου παρουσίαν). The line is from Aeschylus (*Persae* 169), who also gives this title to the royal heir Orestes at *Choephoroe* 934. One thinks also of the title widely applied to the roving minister of the Persian king, who was known as the 'King's Eye'.

The metaphor of the body-politic was of course destined to a long and distinguished development. It is in fact present in the *Republic,* in its metaphors of health and disease. To mention only the most prominent instances: Socrates 'purges' the 'swollen and inflamed' city in Books 2 and 3 (372e, 399e); he compares the rulers to doctors who give the city drugs (459c), compares the collapse of the oligarchic city to the collapse of an unhealthy body into full-blown disease (556e), and the demagogues and their followers to phlegm and bile in the body (564b-c).

Plato's reiterated comparison of the city to a healthy or, more often, a diseased body directs us to what is surely the most important antecedent for the proportional metaphor that underlies the city-soul analogy. The 5th century medical writer Alcmeon describes health as the 'political equality', ἰσονομία, of the body's elements - the hot, the cold, the dry, the wet, the bitter, the sweet, etc. - and sickness as the 'monarchic rule', μοναρχία, of one over the others (fr. B4 Diels-Kranz). Here at last a truly political metaphor - not merely the imagery of power or mastery, κράτος - is used to describe the relations between elements of the person. But they are bodily elements, not psychological. Fill out the proportion implicit in Alcmeon's political metaphor, and this is the result: that if we can think of, say, the bitter element as the ruler of the body, then we can think of rulers as the bitter element of the city. Plato offers us just this sort of expansion of Alcmeon's idea when, substituting Hippocratic humours for Alcmeon's 'hot', 'cold', etc., he compares the disruptive influence of demagogues and their followers in the city to the disruptive influence of phlegm and bile in the body.

In effect, then, the city-soul analogy takes Alcmeon's metaphor for bodily health and sickness and with striking originality applies it to the soul, extrapolates its proportional implications for the city, and for a final twist turns the politics of the metaphor upside-down. For a form of 'monarchy', the rule of the one element that is naturally fit to rule, and not 'political equality' as Alcmeon thought, turns out to be the key to health, whether in the soul or in the city. When Adeimantus comes to describe the democratic soul as that of an ἰσονομικοῦ τινὸς ἀνδρός (561e), 'an "equal-shares" type of fellow', he means it as an insult.

Whether Plato borrowed from Alcmeon only in effect or whether he did so in actual fact is not central to my argument. But like others before me I find it hard not to think that Plato is alluding to Alcmeon at the point where the concept of health is first transferred from body to soul, since he achieves it by having Socrates define health and disease as a condition in which the body's elements 'control and are controlled... *rule and are ruled* (κρατεῖν τε καὶ κρατεῖσθαι... ἄρχειν τε καὶ ἄρχεσθαι) in the way nature does or does not intend' (444d). Here the metaphor of controlling strength familiar from Hippocratics writing on the body and from poets writing on the soul is supplemented by the political metaphor unique to Alcmeon's writing on the body, fresh-minted now for Plato's writing on the soul.

Yet there is one important exception to the rule that psychological forces are not depicted with unambiguously political metaphors before Plato - so important that he takes pains to note it in the *Republic*. Socrates in Book 9 describes the genesis of the tyrannical man as a process in which his soul is usurped by an implanted 'lust' or 'passion', ἔρως. He caps the description with a question: 'Is that the kind of reason, then, why Eros has of old been called a tyrant (τύραννος)?' (573b). Now, the irresistible power of love over men and gods is frequently acknowledged in Greek literature. But only Sophocles writes of Eros 'ruling' (ἄρχει) whomever he pleases (*Trachiniae* 441-44), and only Euripides has come down to us as actually calling Eros a tyrant (τύραννος). He does it twice, in fact: in the *Hippolytus* (538) and in a fragment of the *Andromeda* (fr. 136 Nauck). Since in Book 1 an anecdote is told of the aged and sexually impotent Sophocles' relief at being free of what he calls a 'fierce and mad master (δεσπότην)' (329c), and since in Book 8 Euripides is singled out for his praise of tyranny (568a-b), the question in Book 9 looks to be Plato's acknowledgment of a source and acceptance of a challenge. Let tragedians hymn the tyrant of the soul; Plato will praise its king.

2. Timocracy, oligarchy, democracy

The salient characteristic of a proportional metaphor or simile is its reversibility. Thus the correspondence between city and soul implies both a comparison of the soul to a city (reason is the ruler of the soul) and a comparison of the city to a soul (rulers are the intelligence of the city.) And it does this not simply with the metaphor of reason as ruler of the soul but for each of the elements of our soul, and for every possible relation of power between those elements, both for good and for bad. Although the correspondence is not itself a proportional simile or metaphor, it implies such similes or metaphors at every turn. And it is these points of likeness - not causal relations, nor relations of whole and part - that bind each city to the equivalent soul and each soul to the equivalent city.

We should not go looking for timocratic men in the timocratic city, for example, whether among its ruling class or anywhere else, whether or not we add that such men have turned the city timocratic by projecting their characters upon its constitution. Timocratic man is like a timocracy; he is not a part of one, nor has he made one. Timocracy is like a timocratic man; it does not contain timocratic men, nor was it made by timocratic men. That is, the city-soul analogy makes no determination on these matters.

Detailed consideration of the various forms of unsound society and the correspondingly unsound individuals described in Book 8 will clinch this negative argument. But it will also provide the opportunity for insight into the positive value of the city-soul correspondence - its function in the overall argument of the *Republic.* For the question raised in the previous chapter remains to be answered: If the analyses of the different forms of society and of individual indeed run on parallel but quite separate tracks, what point is there to this duplication?

At first sight, the stage of degeneration nearest to the ideal, that of timocracy and the timocratic man, might seem, despite what has been claimed, to instantiate Williams' predominance rule quite well, and so to offer a grip for externalization. For surely the individual whose soul is led by its spirited part (550b), who loves physical exercise and places high value on the art of war (549a) - the timocratic man - is of the same character as the spirited, warmongering, athletic types who hold power in the timocracy (547e, 548c)? Look closer at these descriptions, however, and it becomes clear that the timocratic man is not some member of the ruling class of the timocratic city picked out of the line-up and placed under individual scrutiny. His character is different from theirs.

One way to see this is in their respective attitudes towards their own money. The rulers of the timocracy are secretive and stingy with their money, and passionate about it (548a-b); the timocratic man, by contrast, begins by being openly contemptuous of it in his youth and ends by openly enjoying it (547d). The explanations are different but analogous, as they should be. In the timocratic city, which is imagined as the first stage of degeneration from Callipolis, the ruling class which used to hold property in common has now divided up the city's wealth and holds property in private (547c). The public and private lives of its members have become dissociated. Publicly, they live as a military elite, gather in common messhalls, and despise commerce and those who must work to make money (547d). Money has become something essentially private for them. In their personal 'nests' they amass it greedily and entertain with it lavishly, in defiance of the law (548a-b).

It is a pathology to be traced from the compromise that generated their constitution. Tension between the intellectual-cum-military values of a degenerate guardian class and the commercial values of the productive class was resolved by abandoning the highest values, the intellectual, which no longer qualify a person for government (547e), by giving public prominence to the military values, which rank next on the scale, and by retaining but subordinating the lowest values, the commercial, making them a purely private matter for its military class (547b-c). (The commercial class, for its part, is reduced to the status of helots and servants; this severity of the city towards its lower class will find its reflection not in the timocratic man's attitude towards money but in his harsh treatment of slaves, 549a.)

The compromise that generates the timocratic man, however, derives from a struggle between his personal values, the elements within his soul; it is no class-struggle. He is driven to hand over control of his soul to its spirited element, its love of honour and victory, as a compromise between adopting his father's lack of political ambition - the rational course in a poorly governed city - and succumbing to the pressure from his mother and the rest of the household to give himself over to the unbridled pursuit of power, status, and wealth (549c-550b). He takes no active role in intellectual pursuits (compare how intellectuals are no longer permitted to rule in a timocracy), but becomes a mere consumer of cultural products (548e). An appetite for wealth does play a significant if subordinate role in his life, as it did in the corresponding city. Differently from the ruling class in the timocracy, however, he has no history of doing without private property. The result is that at no period of his life does he need to be furtive with money and stow it in his private nest; still less does greed lead him to break the law.

In the timocracy, philosophers are no longer in power; it has become a militaristic society - partly modelled on Sparta (545a) - whose discipline is so strict as to be repressive. This brings out furtive behaviour in its rulers, who attempt to evade the law in secret as if running away from a father (548b). But there is no furtiveness in the soul of the timocratic man, although there is some instability. Just as philosophers are no longer guardians in the timocratic society, so the soul of the timocratic man has 'been deprived of the best guardian (τὸ ἀπολειφθῆναι τοῦ ἀρίστου φύλακος)', namely reason (λόγος), its philosophic element (549b). Lacking this guardian, he is not 'purely directed towards virtue' (εἰλικρινὴς πρὸς ἀρετήν); he will not be able to sustain the lordly attitude towards money that he adopted in his youth. The older he gets, the more he will appreciate its value. But at no point will he have to be secretive about it.

A society that puts its military first will require the yoke of strict discipline if military values are to permeate its institutions, and this is likely to show itself in the harshness of its laws. This harshness will then have its effect on the members of its ruling military class. But the equivalent is not true of the individual who is competitive, seeks honour, and admires the art of war. Harsh social restrictions do not mark his life; his character reflects the restrictions of a timocracy from the inside, through its limited range of tastes and enthusiasms and its overall inflexibility (548e). He 'puts his military first' only in the sense that his soul is led by its spirited, aggressive part. He values (ἀξιῶν) the exploits and the art of war as a qualification for ruling; but it is ruling itself, not the art of war, that he is said to love directly (φίλαρχος), along with athletics and hunting (φιλογυμναστής τέ τις ὢν καὶ φιλόθηρος) (549a).

Militarism is not his defining quality. His enthusiasm for hunting, for example, was not a feature of life as described for the rulers of the timocracy, and it presumably corresponds to the value accorded by that society - by the society as a whole, notice, rather than by the members of its military class - to the 'deceptions and stratagems' of war (δόλους τε καὶ μηχανὰς, 548a). The society takes its pleasure in stratagems on a suitably civic scale, in the field of battle; the corresponding man takes his corresponding pleasure out in the field with hare and hounds. (Anyone who doubts that Plato would have thought hunting an appropriate analogue for war and to be associated with deception should look at the closing pages of *Laws* 7, 823b-824a.)

The timocratic man sounds for all the world like a huntin' shootin' fishin' type, a self-important country squire, as it were, though one who seeks influence at court. It is at any rate clear that, once he has coped with the mixed messages sent to him by his family and decided what values will be his guide, he lives a complacent and unconflicted life, quite different from that of the rulers in the timocracy - different not just in its circumstances but in its ethical and psychological tenor.

In the correspondence between timocracy and the timocratic man a factor comes into play that bears comparison with the case of the thoughtful statesman in the previous chapter. If a wise statesman is likely to be a thoughtful person and therefore to know what is good for himself as well as for his society, this likelihood (if such it is) would be grounded in the regularities of human nature. It would be a mistake to justify it by appeal to the city-soul analogy. Similarly, it seems a fact about any society that those of its members who find their vocation in waging war will be spirited, competitive types who live by the honour-code. It may therefore also seem that the rulers of the militaristic timocracy will be timocratic characters, though we have seen they are not; and this misunderstanding may lead to one more general, the view that the city-soul correspondence is shaped by externalization and by the predominance rule.

Plato seems aware of this danger, and takes steps to counteract it. First, he converts the proportional metaphor at work in the correspondence. Not only is the timocratic man a person who 'hands over political power in himself... to the victory-loving and spirited element' (τὴν ἐν ἑαυτῷ ἀρχὴν παρέδωκε τῷ... φιλονίκῳ καὶ θυμοειδεῖ, 550b), but the timocracy is described as exemplifying 'love of victory and honour' (φιλονικίαι καὶ φιλοτιμίαι) by virtue of 'the spirited element that dominates there' (ὑπὸ τοῦ θυμοειδοῦς κρατοῦντος, 548c), where by 'the spirited element' is meant the ruling military class.

This is the one and only time in the *Republic* that Plato explicitly applies the proportional metaphors thrown up by the correspondence in the direction soul-city as well as city-soul. In the next chapter we will see the point of the cast-iron rule this implies. For now, consider instead the effect of Plato's decision to break it here. He puts front and centre what might suggest externalization to the incautious reader: the fact that the spirited element that gives the city its character is a class each member of which is himself spirited (ἄνδρας... θυμοειδεῖς, 547e), and therefore, presumably, dominated by his spirited element.

But Plato has only brought this bombshell to the reader's attention so that he can defuse it in broad daylight. He makes Adeimantus suggest that, so far as the love of victory goes, Glaucon seems a good candidate for the role of timocratic man; only to have Socrates deny it on the grounds that the timocratic man is more stubborn and less cultured than Glaucon (548d-e). Glaucon's love of victory is complicated by other qualities absent in the man who corresponds to the timocracy; and the same is true of the spirited rulers who live in the repressive timocratic regime. Not every spirited person is 'timocratic man'. Plato helps his reader appreciate this by allowing Adeimantus to get the point exactly right: the timocratic man has the 'character of that regime' (ἦθος ἐκείνης τῆς πολιτείας, 549a), not 'the character of the rulers of that regime'; he is the particular character that results when you map the life of the timocratic state onto that of an individual. Not every spirited person has that character, or that life.

But let us follow the correspondence as it steps down the scale of degeneration. Timocracy is succeeded by oligarchy. Here we find that the man who corresponds to the oligarchic society is a hard-working miser (554a), whereas those who rule in an oligarchy - a plutocracy, in which property and wealth qualify a person for power - are simply the rich, indeed the super-rich (ὑπέρπλουτοι, 552b), since so much of the city's wealth is concentrated in so few hands. The class is explicitly said to include the idle, spendthrift rich - the very opposite of the oligarchic man. These spendthrifts are the 'drones', whose habits may eventually impoverish them and cause them to drop from the ruling class (552b-c).

What makes a parsimonious man resemble a plutocracy? Both the individual and the society value material wealth above all (554a-b). In both, only a few of the elements that would find satisfaction in material things are actually allowed to obtain that satisfaction. For the society, this means that wealth is concentrated in the hands of a few, and that the laws encourage this concentration (property can be alienated, 552a); but the same trend is represented in the individual by his striving to limit his material satisfactions to the fewest possible, satisfying only his necessary desires and suppressing the yen for luxuries (554a).

Thus, while the city is conflicted in the sense that rich and poor are hostile to each other, with the rich living in fear of an impoverished and rebellious populace and of a criminal element whom they must hold down by force (551d-e, 552e), the oligarchic man is a conflicted person in his private life. As the city is full of beggars and criminals, so the oligarchic man has many criminal desires, as well as 'beggarly' ones (554c) - whims and longings he considers as worthless to him (554a) as beggars are to the city. Both kinds he suppresses by force, the force of fear. He dreads the financial loss that self-indulgence might impose (554d). But these suppressed longings will come to light if he is given the chance to satisfy them with impunity, as when he mistreats orphans in his care, or spends others' money (554c-d).

It is true that not only the oligarchy itself but the members of its ruling class are described as putting money first, as being 'money-lovers', φιλοχρήματοι

(551e; cf. 551a), and in this respect bear comparison with the oligarchic man (554a vs. 551a, 551e). But it is as with timocratic man and the spirited rulers of the timocracy: not every money-lover has the character of the oligarchic man. The materialism of the oligarchic rulers shows itself in their admiration for the rich and in their unwillingness to fund military campaigns against other cities. But these rulers have no trouble spending money on themselves. Later we are told that their luxurious households and the children that they have accustomed to a permissive lifestyle are a cause of their downfall (556b), a situation that stands in complete contrast to the pinched and illiberal upbringing from which the son of the oligarchic man will escape (558d, 559d). It is the public purse that the rulers of the oligarchy are reluctant to fill. The equivalent in the individual is his unwillingness to spend money on raising himself to prominence in public life (555a). The ruling class in an oligarchy, however, are socially prominent already; the prominence they are unwilling to bankroll is that of their city among other cities. Their military campaigns are underfunded, and they are in any case afraid to arm the rebellious populace; so they go into battle, by a nice pun, as ὀλιγαρχικοί in the true sense of the word: not just 'the few in command' but 'in command of few' (551e).

The same pun yields quite different results when applied to the oligarchic man. The reason he is unwilling to spend money on making his mark in public life is that he fears giving power to the hitherto suppressed rabble of his lavish desires, desires which could support political ambition (555a). Success in public life tends to require emotional resources that the oligarchic man cannot muster in himself: lavishness in the cause of self-promotion, and a willingness to be smitten by the excitement of the social scene. So he brings only a small part of himself to the political arena, goes into combat ὀλιγαρχικῶς, that is, 'half-heartedly' - and keeps hold of his money. Stinginess in him is derived from an inner starvation and an inner conflict quite absent from what we are told about the ruling class in the oligarchy. Nor is the description of the oligarchic man a supplement to that of the rulers in the oligarchy, offering the glimpse inside the soul of those rulers that was missing from the analysis of their public role. For it is an analysis that shows those rulers living in a way no oligarchic man could countenance.

Once again, a comment from Adeimantus helps keep the reader on course. As with each of the unsound types, the character of the oligarchic man is formed in part by his having a father whose character is one step higher on the moral scale. Socrates imagines the timocratic father coming to grief in his pursuit of political power and impoverishing his family as a result. The son, who had until then been following in his father's footsteps, now avoids political risk and concentrates on making money (553a-d). Adeimantus agrees that such circumstances would be most likely to turn 'an ambitious young man into an avaricious one' (ἐκ φιλοτίμου νέου εἰς φιλοχρήματον). Socrates pursues the matter:

> 'And is this the oligarchic (ὀλιγαρχικός) type?'
> 'Well, he certainly develops from the kind of man who is like the regime from which oligarchy developed.'
> 'Let's see, then, if he will be like the oligarchic regime'. (553e)

Adeimantus chooses his words carefully. The young man that Socrates described has clearly turned into a lover of money (φιλοχρήματος), but what exactly does Socrates mean by calling him 'oligarchic'? The word ὀλιγαρχικός would normally describe a person whose political views favour oligarchy. But Adeimantus is aware that Socrates is not analysing the political views of the individuals who correspond to the various types of city so much as their moral characters and their ways of life. He appreciates, too, that the correspondences between city and individual run on parallel but quite separate tracks. Even if it were likely that a young man who puts money first would favour the politics of an oligarchy - or at least of one that has been defined as plutocratic (550c) - that likelihood would be irrelevant to the question whether he should be called 'oligarchic' in the sense demanded by the correspondence. The only way to justify the label is to make out the correspondence, to draw the points of analogy. And the only likelihood that supports the justification so far derives from the parallel progress of that correspondence - from the fact that, just as oligarchy had its origin in timocracy, so the money-loving young man had his analogous 'origin' in a father who resembles a timocracy. It is likely, then, that he will turn out to resemble an oligarchy and merit the title 'oligarchic' - not because of his probable politics but because Adeimantus trusts that the analogy will work out.

Notice, finally, that although the timocracy, with its secretly rich military men and grumbling helots, is no less sharply divided among rich and poor than is the oligarchy, it was not described as two cities, a city of the rich and a city of the poor, as oligarchy is (551d). This is because the city that is two cities corresponds to a man who lives a conflicted, repressed life; but the timocratic man, we saw, is quite unconflicted; if anything, it is the ruling class in the timocracy that lives the conflicted life.

All in all, the oligarchic individual is going to be a little man, a private man, one who makes no impression in public life. He will be a socially respectable - if secretly lascivious - hard-saving, hard-working businessman or productive labourer of some sort. As such, he need bear little resemblance to anyone who qualifies to rule in an oligarchy, where the ruling class manifest a different aspect of materialism (τὸ φιλοχρήματον): not the amassing of money for few personal uses, few avenues of expenditure, but a political preference for minimising taxes and keeping wealth in the hands of the wealthy, amassing money for few people in the city to spend.

The case of democracy and the democratic man is the one that Williams brought to our attention. Democracy is the society in which people are given the opportunity to arrange their lives as they please, and so - human nature being what it is - the democratic state will contain a wide variety of characters, living quite different types of lives (557b-c). But the democratic man has a style of life peculiar to himself: he follows his whim, and leaps from one enthusiasm to the next. The democratic man is one who loves variety; democracy is a society that permits a variety of lifestyles. What in the society is simultaneous variety becomes consecutive variety in the corresponding man; after all, it is more difficult for an individual than for a city to contain multitudes. Accordingly, were the ruling class of a democracy - whether construed as all the people, or the large majority - to consist of democratic types, the variety of democratic society would vanish.

One could attempt to salvage its variety by arguing, for example, that a society of democratic characters would contain many different lifestyles at any particular moment because most of its whimsical citizens would simultaneously be following different whims. The attempt might find encouragement in the epithet common to the citizens of the democracy and the democratic man: not only the city but its citizens are 'free', ἐλεύθεροι (557b), and this too is the boast of the democratic man, that his life is 'sweet, free (ἐλευθέριον), and blessed' (561d). But we should be as careful in this instance as when examining timocracy and oligarchy not to permit a shared epithet to mask important differences.

The freedom experienced by the citizens of the democracy is political. It is a matter of not tolerating limits that the city might impose on their public conduct, nor considering oneself bound by civic obligations. In fact it seems closer to 'anarchy' than to freedom (πολιτεία... ἄναρχος, 558c), and to the extent that it portrays democracy at Athens is certainly intended as a caricature rather than as an accurate account. The city may neither compel you to take up public office nor set qualifications for public office should you choose to seek it; may neither impose military or jury service on you nor punish you for ignoring the decisions of its courts (558a-c). But this is not at all the kind of freedom that characterizes the democratic man. The restrictions and obligations he refuses to acknowledge are restrictions on his personal desires and on what would conventionally be thought of as his obligations to himself. Convention dictates that a true gentleman ought to value only some among his desires, while restraining others (561b-c). This is conduct he owes to himself, not to his city. But the democratic man refuses to brook conventional limits on his conception of himself. He assigns equal value to each of his desires, and gratifies the desire of the moment. The equivalent in the democracy is its refusal to be influenced by considerations of social rank - valuing equal and unequal citizens alike (558c) - and its assigning public office by lot (557a).

Maintaining the separation between the twin tracks of the analogy allows us to appreciate that there is nothing whimsical about citizens' lives in the democracy, as there is about the life of the democratic man. The citizens of the democracy are jealous of their freedoms, and resolute in their resistance to any attempt to infringe those freedoms (563c-d). Even when the discussion turns to how their political freedom influences their domestic and private lives - a turn the discussion takes only in order to explain how democracy degenerates into tyranny, and not because the analogy requires examination of the private lives of ruling classes - this influence manifests itself not in whimsical behaviour but in the breakdown of domestic hierarchy, with fathers afraid of their sons, teachers of their students, and an absence of discipline according to distinctions of rank between husband and wife, master and servant, even master and dog (562e-563d).

The democratic man is resolute too, in a way: 'he sticks to his way of life through everything' (χρῆται αὐτῷ [sc. τὸν βίον τοῦτον] διὰ παντός, 561d). But what he sticks to is a life 'without order or necessity' (οὔτε τις τάξις οὔτε ἀνάγκη, 561d). He is consistently inconsistent, passionately committed to being flighty. This is not at all the kind of freedom that the citizens of the democracy are passionate about. And the difference between freedoms derives from the difference between levels of the city-soul correspondence. When citizens insist too much on their civic freedom, it is their city that becomes anarchic; but when it is each desire within one man that must be free, the anarchy will reign in his soul, not his city.

It will come as no surprise by now that Adeimantus has a careful comment to make on this limb of the correspondence too. He praises Socrates' description of the temporary enthusiasms that succeed each other in the democratic man's life as 'an excellent account of the life of an "equal-shares" sort of fellow (ἰσονομικοῦ τινος ἀνδρός)' (561e). Ἰσονομία was, in complicated ways, a watchword of democratic politics, and the citizens of a democracy were pleased to call themselves ἰσόνομοι; but the adjective ἰσονομικός is apparently attested only here. We saw that Adeimantus hesitated to apply the political term ὀλιγαρχικός to the oligarchic man; δημοκρατικός, likewise, would normally describe a person who favours a democratic constitution. Adeimantus wisely prefers to invent a term that has no currency in political debate, and plays on its political allusiveness in order to describe, not the democratic man's political views, but his crusade to secure equal rights for his every whim. When he proceeds to allow Socrates to call this man 'democratic in the proper sense of the word' (ὡς δημοκρατικὸς ὀρθῶς ἂν προσαγορευόμενος, 562a), he does so because the proper sense of the word has turned out to be a new sense of the word.

A final detail stands in the path of those who would people the democracy with democratic types. The proposal cannot be made to fit with the division of this society into three classes: the rich, the drones, and the general populace (564d-565a). It is a division that Socrates makes in order to explain how democracy degenerates into tyranny. Democratic man would not be at home in any of these three classes, as they are described. Not among the rich, because in a democracy it is those with 'the most disciplined temperament' who become the wealthiest (κοσμιώτατοι φύσει, 564e); not among the drones, because a dronish character is ruled by his unnecessary desires (559c-d), whereas democratic man gives equal rights to each of his desires (561a-b); and not even among the populace, because the populace consists of manual workers and small-time farmers with little money and no time for politics (565a) - with no leisure or resources, then, to support the lifestyle of a democratic man, whose ever-changing enthusiasms take him in and out of the public sphere.

3. Why metaphors matter

The reader of Book 8 confronts a series of parallel indictments of civic and personal ways of life, each imagined in vivid and often satirical detail, each linked to its partner by a complex network of points of likeness. But the more vivid and particular - not to say peculiar - the portraits of these cities and these men become, the less it may seem that they matter. The description of democratic man, for example, is both amusing and immediately recognizable; but why is the unsatisfactoriness of *this* particular manner of living selected for our attention, when there are so many other unsatisfactory ways of living that merit condemnation? The apparent answer is that this is the man whose character resembles that of a democracy. But the answer only generates further questions. We must assume that Plato knew where he was headed when he devised the city-soul analogy. He did not simply fasten on the major types of political constitution and let the analogy take him where it might with the corresponding types of individual. For one thing, those constitutions are not analysed as political systems; the focus is not on their institutions and structures, their balance of power, their laws, or on any of the terms of political analysis that we find in a work such as Aristotle's *Politics*.

Some details, certainly, fit a more technical legislative mould; for example, the proposal that, where property is alienable, contracts should be undertaken at one's own risk (556a-b), a proposal that reappears in the *Laws* (e.g. 742c). The focus, however, is not on such matters, but on these cities' moral character, on their civic values and civic life. Besides, as Norbert Blössner has pointed out, one of their number, 'timocracy', was not a standard constitutional form at all, and did not figure in contemporary constitutional debate.[10] (Socrates makes a fuss about having to invent the name, 545b.) Another, oligarchy, was by no means standardly defined as the rule of the rich rather than the rule of the few. Plato selects the types of constitution with one eye on the individual types that the correspondence will yield, and with the ultimate aim of arriving at a suitable indictment of the tyrannical man.

But it does not seem right to insist that he is looking exclusively in one or other direction - whether determining the types of soul on the basis of landmarks in the domain of constitutional types or conversely determining what will count as a landmark among constitutional types on the basis of what seem to him fundamental types of soul. The correspondences are proportional, and it is characteristic of proportions to be symmetrical.

[10] Blössner 1997, 88.

Plato would be losing half his analogy's usefulness if he were not filling each pan of the scales with a view to what he wishes to place in the other.

So I propose to take more or less at face-value Socrates' claim to have selected the types of constitution that fall into conspicuously definable categories (544c). To be sure, they are moral or behavioural categories rather than the technical political categories they might at first seem, but as such they are true to the reality of Greek politics. Militarism, materialism, and the drive for equality, to consider just the three that have occupied us in this chapter, are not badly-chosen values to apply to the analysis of the tensions in Greek society both within and between states. Even if none of the portraits of civic life reflects the life of a historical community with complete accuracy but each is the caricature of a tendency found in actual communities, sometimes simultaneously, as with oligarchic and democratic factions at Athens, this is not to deny these caricatures a genuinely political application. Likewise, even though not every spirited person is timocratic man, nor every materialist oligarchic man, those Theophrastean vignettes turn on and make concrete distinctions between basic human motivations and desires that reappear elsewhere in Plato's dialogues, and which are of broader application than the vignettes themselves.

This is to describe the independent value of each side of the proportion, its respective indictments of the varieties of civic life and of the varieties of individual ways of life. But what of its value as an analogy? Take first the mapping of city onto soul. The lives of individuals are more familiar to us than the complex lives of cities; we can more readily grasp individual lives as wholes and, if need be, condemn them. Compressing the moral character of a city into the compass of a single human soul invites us to see whole and at a stroke what we normally would not see whole and at a stroke. Compare the bird's eye view we get of Italy's coastline by speaking of it as a 'boot'. If a timocracy were a man, it would be a pompous, complacent squire; if an oligarchy were a man, it would be a blinkered, conflicted miser; if a democracy were a man, it would be a hopeless lightweight. Anyone attracted to these regimes is encouraged by the analogy to consider them whole and not imagine themselves as members of a privileged class within it. When projecting Callipolis Socrates insists that his task is to make the whole city as happy as possible, not some particular class (420b). But it is difficult to grasp the happiness or indeed the unhappiness of an entire city when one is describing its various groups, some of whom may be more content with their lot than others. The mapping of city onto soul helps us achieve this grasp.

Consider now the converse, the mapping of soul onto city. Rather than enable us to see whole what we had previously looked at piecemeal, this mapping enables us to appreciate complications that the more obvious unity of the individual may have masked. The idea is no longer to look at Italy's boot but at the toe and heel and leg of that boot. It is all too easy for an individual to ignore his own needs and desires, to deal with the immediately pressing demands and tensions of the society in which he moves and pass over the demands and tensions within himself. But project those needs and desires onto the big screen of the city - Socrates speaks rather of reading the same letters written both big and small (368d) - and each acquires a voice that cannot be ignored. The same human inclination to concentrate on the middle ground of one's actions as an individual within society to the exclusion, on the one side, of one's inner life, and on the other, of the life of the society as a whole, now works to make that inner life apparent in just the way that, when mapping city onto soul, it allowed us to grasp the civic life.

Plato contrives to make this point by having Adeimantus and Glaucon display the inclination in question. When Socrates has to insist that his task is to make the whole city as happy as possible, rather than any particular class within it, he is responding to complaints first from Adeimantus (419a) and later from his brother (519d-e) on behalf of the ruling class of Callipolis. Adeimantus is concerned that Socrates is being unfair to the guardians, giving them all the duties and none of the privileges of rule; Glaucon is concerned that Socrates is being unfair to the philosophers, making them sacrifice part of their life to governing when they could devote the whole of it to the nobler pursuit of philosophy.

They are forgetting that Socrates is not only describing civic arrangements that have an intrinsic interest (though he is surely doing that too), he is fashioning an analogue for the just individual. They give the ruling class of Callipolis a voice, hear quite clearly the reservations that it might express, but have not heard the voice of the corresponding element within the philosopher, the yearning of his philosophic part for true blessedness, and the reserve it feels about the politics of the soul. They are slow to do this despite being very ready to consider the inner life of the individual, despite having themselves directed Socrates to consider justice in terms of that inner life, and despite Adeimantus' demonstrating a clear grasp of how the analogy works when it comes to timocracy, oligarchy, and democracy. The explanation lies in the difficulty the brothers find in conceiving that health of the soul could be a staging-post rather than the end of our journey towards happiness, as we saw at the end of chapter 1. Projecting the philosopher's soul onto the screen of Callipolis gives them - and through them, the reader - a way to overcome that difficulty.

Projecting soul onto city is no less illuminating when it comes to the unsound characters of Book 8. The life of a democratic man may seem free, relaxed, and various, and therefore enviable (561d-e); but project it onto the democratic city and it is revealed as merely anarchic. Those who envy the democratic man are looking only at his behaviour as an individual moving in society, and in this domain the equality of his desires manifests itself as a sequence. The exercise of one whim follows the exercise of another; he cannot be roaring drunk and piously sober at once, however much he might like to try the experience. In the city, however, the equality of citizens is simultaneous, and results in general lawlessness and mutual contempt. And the point that this projection reveals is: Within his soul, the democratic man *is* roaring drunk and piously sober at once. Outwardly he may make it through life well enough in his whimsical fashion, with help from his friends, perhaps, or from his trust fund, or with plain good luck. Inwardly, his soul is a chaos. The projection allows us similarly to penetrate the oligarchic man's superficial respectability (554d-e), or the timocratic man's superficial nobility (549b).

In effect, the symmetrical correspondence of city and soul, soul and city, contains instruction on how to live in society. (Proclus thought Plato was trying to be Homer; but Plato was surely looking over his shoulder at Hesiod quite as often as he looked to Homer.) The correspondence recommends a joint awareness of political macrocosm and microcosm, of society and of self as organized wholes, at the expense of one's habitual focus on self in society, self in relation to others. It could not do so if it attempted to be more than an analogy and show us the democratic man living in the democratic city, or the just man living in the just city.

Nevertheless each of us is, of course, a person living in a society, and if the analogy does not consider the just man living in the just city, the *Republic* certainly does. It shows us the philosopher living in Callipolis (498e). And the philosopher in Callipolis exemplifies precisely the awareness recommended by the analogy. He is disposed to rule out of concern for the good of society as a whole, not for his rank within it - this is his awareness of the political macrocosm. He is disposed to maintain the health of his soul, in all its aspects, because he is aware that he is only human – or rather, sees what is human in him as well as what is godlike. He is doctor of his soul for this reason, because he sees himself as a microcosm, and not because he seeks to be a gentleman and to merit the mantle of kingship. And his disposition to philosophize? He does philosophy simply because he loves it. But this love is not Plato's main concern with the philosopher in the *Republic;* his concern with the philosopher in this dialogue is rather for how he should live in society.

To say that the philosopher-king exemplifies the awareness recommended by the analogy is not, however, to say that he would justify that awareness by the analogical reasoning contained in the city-soul correspondence. The lesson of that correspondence is directed at readers of the *Republic,* not at the philosopher-kings.

But we will return in the next chapter to the philosopher's attitude toward the politics of his city and of his soul and examine it more closely. Here let us note instead how, by being an analogy and nothing more, the city-soul correspondence complies with Glaucon's and Adeimantus' demand to leave out the rewards and consequences of justice and injustice and examine only their effects on the soul - complies with this demand and at the same time escapes its limits. Because the analogy does nothing to place the varieties of individual in the societies to which they correspond but considers each individual as a self-contained microcosm, it successfully abstracts from external rewards and consequences. Because, however, the analogue for each individual is a city, a civic way of life, Socrates is also able to praise and indict justice and injustice in the more conventional social application of these terms that the brothers' demand might seem to have excluded. And because, finally, commendation of a way to live in society is implied by the very workings of the analogy, and that political stance, as we have just seen, turns out to do away with external rewards and consequences not by rejecting them or abstracting from them but simply by rising above them, Socrates offers the brothers an alternative to the corrosive aspect of quietism, its retreat from the social world, its licking of wounds, yet preserves the positive aspect - its focus on the politics of the soul - even as he pursues an ideal that can reconnect the brothers to the prospect of kingship. This last would be the reason why Plato scripted the brothers' demand to begin with. Writing around its constraint enables him to explain how one should live in society, and this is what in the *Republic* he set out to do.

If all this is correct, then one function can be excluded from the repertoire of the city-soul analogy: it is not genuinely heuristic, no matter what Socrates may suggest to the contrary (434d-e; a passage to which we shall return). As an analogy it is genuinely illuminating, in the way that metaphors can be. But we are not to imagine Plato listing in one column what seem to him the fundamental types of good and bad constitution, then performing the metaphorical calculations that will produce the corresponding types of good and bad individual, wondering all the while what will turn up in the other column. Nor should we imagine him trying it the other way round. The various matches are too clearly tailored to fit in advance. What Plato uses the analogy for is not discovery, but communication with the reader.

Consideration of the three correspondences between city and soul completed in Book 8 has confirmed that the analogy is based neither on Williams' predominance rule nor on Lear's reshaping of it as an externalization rule. But could a different reshaping of the predominance rule lie behind the analogy? Granted that a timocracy is not conceived as the society ruled by timocratic men, nor an oligarchy as the society ruled by oligarchic types, could we not at least say that timocracy is the society among whose ruling class timocratic man aspires to belong, and likewise with oligarchy and democracy? We might be encouraged in this thought by a statement Socrates makes about democracy: that it is 'for any man of free spirit (ὅστις φύσει ἐλεύθερος), the only place worth living in' (562c).

There is no need to deny that each type of man, to the extent that he has the character of the city to which he corresponds, would presumably find that city a congenial place to live, and if he lived there would presumably wish to belong to its elite - not because its members have his character, but because most people think it better to have power than to lack it, and because he would want to ensure that the city remains the congenial place that attracted him in the first place. But it is important to deny that the analogy is in any sense grounded on such a principle, or constructed so as to express it. Socrates' statement about democracy is actually a report of the slogan that proud citizens of democracies like to bandy among themselves, and crops up in his analysis of how democracy degenerates into tyranny. It forms no part of his description of democratic man, and is not presented as an account of that man's relation to democracy.

It bears pointing out also that the ambitions of the various unsound types of individual would all be most completely satisfied not in cities of corresponding character but in a tyranny. None is more exalted and worshipped than the tyrant, none amasses greater wealth, none is more free to act on his whims, for he brooks no competition in these matters. Timocracy, oligarchy, and democracy do not, then, make concrete the ambitions of timocratic, oligarchic, and democratic man, nor are these constitutions described, as Blössner believes,[11] for the sake of demonstrating the unsoundness of those ambitions. They are described partly for their own sake, partly for the sake of clarifying by analogy the inner condition of the corresponding man, and not at all for the sake of realizing his dreams.

Only when it comes to the man of tyrannical character does Plato announce this theme, and only outside the terms of the city-soul analogy. It is a defining feature of the tyrannical character, and is not of any other, to dream of bending an entire society to his individual needs and desires. So it is by breaking the mould of the city-soul analogy that Plato exhibits this character. The externalization rule does not apply to the city-soul analogy, it applies to the tyrannical character who becomes an actual tyrant. The predominance rule does not apply to the city-soul analogy, it applies to philosophers in Callipolis. Let us see how, and why.

[11] Blössner 1997, 91-92, 204.

Sources and Scholarly Contexts for Chapter 3

The CD-ROM (Version 'E') of the *Thesaurus Linguae Graecae* proved an indispensable tool for investigating the psychological metaphors that Plato inherited. And it is a pleasure to acknowledge the use I also made of the dissertation 'The Divided Self from Homer to Aristotle' (1997) that David Engel wrote at Berkeley under my supervision. When it came to the psychological metaphors used in Greek tragedy the work of Shirley Darcus Sullivan saved me much labour (Darcus Sullivan 1997, 1999, 2000).

Alcmeon's importance as ancestor of the political metaphors that Plato applies to the soul is placed in historical context in Cambiano 1982 and Vegetti ed., 1998 [vol. 3], p. 102 n. 122 (and compare Vegetti 1983, ch. 2). I differ from both scholars in not treating metaphorical uses of κράτος and κρατεῖν as fully political.

The tendency in current scholarship to suppose that the ruling class of a timocracy will consist of timocratic individuals, that of an oligarchy, of oligarchic individuals, and so on, was documented in 'Sources and scholarly contexts for chapter 2'.

By taking the view that the two sides of the analogy have independent political and psychological value I put myself at variance with several positions currently in the field. While accepting the arguments in Blössner 1997, pp. 185-207 and Frede 1997 against the historicity of the political arrangements represented in the unjust societies, I do not accept that this renders those portraits politically irrelevant. Still less do I take this as an argument that renders the *Republic* as a whole politically irrelevant, turning it into an exclusively moral work, *pace* Annas 1999, p. 77. Nor do I follow Blössner 1997, pp. 215-16, 241 in denying that the analogy is intended to contain a Platonic psychology - despite agreeing with him that the analogy is not intended as heuristic. Let us say by all means that Plato adapts his psychological concepts to the needs of the dialogues in which they appear; but let us recognize also that once allowance has been made for context enough remains constant between a significant number of dialogues to warrant talk of a Platonic 'psychology'.

CHAPTER 4

Tyrant and King

1. An asymmetry

When it comes to two of the individuals who resemble particular cities, the philosopher and the tyrannical man, and only when it comes to those two, the *Republic* goes beyond describing analogical relations between man and city to show us the man ruling in the city and the effects of that position on his character. It considers in those two instances the causal relations that are so strikingly absent from the operation of the analogy proper. Another detour through rhetorical observations on metaphor will help us reach an explanation.

We have seen that proportional metaphors are convertible and that the correspondence between society and individual is, accordingly, as much a soul-city as a city-soul analogy. But it is time to qualify these claims. To say that a proportional metaphor is convertible is not to guarantee that it will make an equally effective metaphor in either direction. Aristotle, despite appreciating the convertibility of such metaphors, does not draw attention to this fact; but later rhetoricians made it explicit.

The example in the previous chapter involving general, charioteer, and helmsman, quoted from 'Demetrius' *On Style* (78), is followed in that treatise by an example, no less proportional, that does not convert in the same way: poets call the 'lower slope' (ὑπώρεια) of Mt. Ida its 'foot' (πούς), but do not call a man's foot his lower slope; so 'not all [such metaphors] convert'. An anonymous treatise *On Tropes* (*Rhetores Graeci* ed. Spengel, vol. 3 p. 228) draws the same conclusion from a line about an island 'garlanded' by the boundless sea. Water that flows around an island can be said to garland it, but to describe a garland as 'flowing around' someone's head would be 'laughable' (τὸ γὰρ τοιοῦτον γελοῖον). Likewise, when Thrasymachus restates in proportional terms the idea that the king is shepherd of his people (343b), he achieves his sardonic effect by casting the dignified old metaphor in the reflected light of its undignified converse, that the shepherd is king of his sheep.

Now, there is nothing obviously laughable about describing rulers as the intelligence of their city, or soldiers as its spirit; one may even think of farmers and artisans, since they make it possible for the city to feed itself, as the city's hunger and thirst. It is certainly no more strange than to call a king the eye of his household, or to compare demagogues to phlegm and bile. Nevertheless, Plato inherited (with the one exception noted in the previous chapter) only the second sort of comparison from his culture, comparisons between elements of the city and those of the human body, but not those of the human soul. And we also saw that, when it comes to the bodily metaphors, he makes a point of running the proportion in both directions: not only is ill-health like misrule, but demagogues are like phlegm and bile; not only does a doctor rule his patient's body, but rulers are doctors of the city.

He could easily have done the same with metaphors of the soul. He was no prisoner of inherited imagery. Yet he does not do it. And the fact that he does not is therefore significant; he must have chosen not to. His text is replete with political imagery applied to the soul. Reason is a ruler who deliberates on behalf of the community of soul-parts, and attempts to prevent civil strife among them. And what of that *tour de force* in Book 8, when Socrates evokes the popular revolution that turns the soul of a young man democratic (560a-561a)? The mob seize reason's citadel, bar its gates to wise advice, and celebrate the triumph of licence with a torchlit parody of the Eleusinian Mysteries. Yet although the correspondence between city and soul, being symmetrical, suggests any number of metaphors or similes that could be applied in the opposite direction, none is made explicit.

Rulers are never called the 'reasoning part' (λογιστικόν) of the city, or even the 'wisdom' (σοφία) of the city; soldiers, with the one exception in Book 8 (548c) that I mentioned in the preceding chapter, are not called the city's 'spirit' (θυμός) or 'spirited element' (θυμοειδές), or its 'courage' (ἀνδρεία), nor are farmers and artisans ever called the city's 'desiring part' (ἐπιθυμητικόν), any more than the ruling class in an oligarchy is described as the city's 'necessary desires' (ἀναγκαῖαι ἐπιθυμίαι) or the tyrant as its 'lust' (ἔρως). Instead, the pervasive imagery applied to the city's constituents is more traditional, and derives either from medicine - the classes in the city are elements of a diseased body - or from the animal realm - the city is a hive, the demagogues its drones (552c, 564b); the tyrant is a man who turns into a wolf (566a).

It seems, then, that Plato takes advantage of the sequence in which the analogy is explained - having Socrates describe first the structure of the city, then that of the corresponding soul - in order to avoid applying his proportional metaphors in both directions. He applies them in one direction only, the same direction in which he presents the correspondence. One could, of course, take this as evidence supporting the claim that the constitutional arrangements and ways of life in Callipolis and the unjust types of city are after all intended as nothing more than images of corresponding structures and ways of life in the individual. But then we would be left with the problem of explaining why the complexity of those images, especially but not only that of Callipolis, goes so far beyond what is required for the comparison. And more decisively, if these are nothing more than images of personal morality, we would be compelled to ignore the political implications that they so clearly have - their effectiveness as praise or as indictment of the varieties of civic life.

There is a better way to explain why Plato applies the metaphors thrown up by the city-soul correspondence in an asymmetrical fashion. There is an ethical position he intends to contest, involving a relation between soul and city that is at once analogical and causal. Asymmetrical application of these metaphors is one of the ways in which he realizes his intention. The matching of tyrant and philosopher at the extremes of the city-soul correspondence is another.

The position derives from an idea that neither Plato nor, probably, anyone else would want to contest: the idea that those in authority should lead by example. We find in Xenophon's *Memorabilia* (3.2.2) the thought that a good king not only orders his own life well but also makes his subjects flourish, and in his *Cyropaedia* (1.6.8) the thought that a king must be superior to his subjects not so much in his luxurious lifestyle as in forethought and in his appetite for work. In Stobaeus' collection of maxims, assembled in the time of the late Roman empire, this one is considered sufficiently venerable to be attributed to Thales: 'Ruler, put yourself in order' (ἄρχων κόσμει σεαυτόν, Diels-Kranz 1.64.10). Here an implication of the uncontroversial idea is clearer: that it is by ruling yourself that you become worthy to rule others.

But nor is this the thought that Plato wishes to contest. Indeed, he puts a strong formulation of it on Socrates' lips at the climax of his response to Glaucon's challenge: those who do not have the 'divine ruler' (θεῖον ἄρχον) within their own souls should for their own good be ruled by those who do - should in fact be their slaves (590c-d). But take the thought one step further, suggest not only that self-rule makes one worthy to rule others but that ruling others is its finest expression, since political rule is the greatest task a man can undertake, and you have the thought that Plato wished to contest. His philosopher, even the philosopher who becomes king, has a greater ambition than that.

Significantly, the contestable pattern of thought can be found in an early work of Isocrates, his *To Nicocles*, written probably in the late 370s. It is a work of moral counsel addressed to the Cyprian king, and contains in section 29 the following advice: to be truly kingly (βασιλικώτατος), the king must be no slave to pleasure (ἂν μηδεμιᾷ δουλεύῃς τῶν ἡδονῶν) but must take his own desires more firmly in control than he controls his citizens (κρατῇς τῶν ἐπιθυμιῶν μᾶλλον ἢ τῶν πολιτῶν); for it is self-rule that gives him the right to rule others (ἄρχε σαυτοῦ μηδὲν ἧττον ἢ τῶν ἄλλων). Thus far, the extra step has not been taken; Isocrates has not said much more than he does in *To Demonicus* 21 (if this is indeed his work): a person who has self-control (ἐγκράτεια) thinks it shameful to hold authority over slaves while being a slave to pleasures (ἐὰν αἰσχρὸν ὑπολάβῃς τῶν μὲν οἰκετῶν ἄρχειν, ταῖς δ᾽ἡδοναῖς δουλεύειν). What makes for the extra step is the claim that 'kingship... is the greatest (μέγιστον) of human activities, and requires the most care' (*To Nicocles* 6). For this is to suggest that there is no finer consequence of one's self-rule than that it qualifies one to rule others.

If you wish to rule others, and to be worthy of ruling them, first rule yourself: this is what Isocrates, Plato's great rival, taught the members of the elite, both native and foreign, who came to his school to learn what he did not hesitate to call 'philosophy' (φιλοσοφία). And the only motives he could imagine for their perhaps *not* wishing to rule others were the dangers and anxieties that accompany supreme office (*To Nicocles* 5, *Letter to the Sons of Jason* 11-12). He did not give them something yet finer than supreme office to which they might aspire.

Isocrates' advice implies a familiar correspondence between city and soul: as the ruler's controlling part stands to his own desires, so he, the ruler, stands to his citizens. But there is a causal rather than purely analogical connection at work. The ruler's control over himself is presented as justifying his actual control over the society, for it is the self-ruled king that will rule his society well. The analogical thought is grounded in a causal one: that the society will not be structured within itself as the ruler is structured within himself unless a ruler of that very type is in control of it. It is a version of what we have been calling the predominance rule. One who holds this view of the relation between soul and city in the well-run society would be sympathetic to the idea that successful rulers shape society in their own image, make it a likeness of their inner politics. He would be sympathetic, in other words, to the idea that successful rulers manage to externalize themselves, in Jonathan Lear's sense of that term. Isocrates does not disappoint this expectation. 'Make your self-discipline (σωφροσύνη) an example to the rest', he says, pursuing his counsel to King Nicocles, 'knowing that the character of the city as a whole resembles its rulers (τὸ τῆς πόλεως ὅλης ἦθος ὁμοιοῦται τοῖς ἄρχουσιν)' (*To Nicocles* 31). Thus the misunderstandings of the city-soul correspondence considered in chapter 2 turn out not simply to be modern misreadings of the *Republic* but misreadings that are thematized and contested within the *Republic* itself.

By applying in an asymmetrical fashion the metaphors that derive from the correspondence, Plato indicates his lack of sympathy with what we can now call the Isocratean idea. We saw at the close of the previous chapter how he uses the analogy between soul and city to seize on a natural inclination to concentrate on the middle ground of one's individual actions in society and redirect this inclination towards a dual focus on the extremes, on individual microcosm and social macrocosm. Isocrates uses the same analogy but follows the natural inclination. Unlike Plato, he is counseling a king on how to deserve his social position. His focus is on the king's actions as an individual moving in society; and since that individual is the king, the focus is on actions that give the society its character. Self-discipline is surely something praiseworthy in itself, making the king a good person as well as a good king; but the point of the king's being a good person, so far as Isocrates' homily is concerned, is that he can thereby be a good king and make a good society.

Plato, by contrast, has Socrates concentrate the metaphorical energy of the city-soul correspondence entirely on the individual soul, not on the city, and thereby bring his listeners' moral and emotional energy to that same focus. For although the city-soul correspondence is itself symmetrical, and although many of its moral and political lessons emerge from this symmetry, there remains a way in which the *Republic* does after all focus on soul rather than city and exalt the individual over society. Not that the

Republic is only a moral and not also a political work; but it recognizes that the city is capable of less than the man. The city at its best is free from strife, stable, and harmonious; its productivity is kept so far as possible on a continuous cycle. The city at its best supports its philosophic class; but except in this sense, the city does not philosophize. Only individual philosophers can do that. The individual at his best is not only harmonious of soul but capable of philosophy, and it is philosophy, not kingship, that is the highest human achievement. The philosopher's productivity, his fertility of soul, is not cyclical but progressive, taking him ever closer to god. Justice, accordingly, amounts to something more in the man than in the city, despite being an analogous order of analogous elements in both. This is possible simply because a man is something more than a city.

My argument does not hang on identifying Isocrates as the source of the approach that Plato resists. We cannot even be certain that composition of *To Nicocles* preceded that of the *Republic,* and it may be that Isocrates is resisting Plato rather than vice versa. What can be said with confidence is that no contemporary of Plato so directly addresses the correspondence between the very structure of the king's soul, on the one hand, and the structure of his relation to his subjects, on the other, as does Isocrates in the passage from *To Nicocles,* with its reference to the king's rule over his own desires.

We have also seen the Isocratean pattern of thought at work in a passage considered in an earlier chapter, when Glaucon pressed a reluctant Socrates to describe the city's self-discipline, and Socrates, unusually, explained the city's virtue by first describing the virtue of the individual (431c-d). The result was much what we find in Isocrates: the city can only be called self-disciplined if those who seem to be self-disciplined themselves - those whose appetites, due to superior birth and breeding, are simple and amenable to the guidance of good sense - are in control of their inferiors, and of the many and various appetites found among them. It is in this passage that Plato thematizes most revealingly his resistance to the Isocratean thought, just before presenting his own development of the city-soul analogy. Let us reconsider it with this in mind.

Socrates does not actually call the members of the superior class self-disciplined, and we saw in chapter 2 that Plato ensures that he does not speak of the behaviour of individuals but rather of the pleasures and tastes of whole classes. The good sense to which the best born and bred are amenable need not, after all, be the individual good sense of each. And even to the extent that the account of the city's self-discipline implies that the members of its ruling class will, in general, be self-disciplined, this is not because the analogy demands it - not, then, because the predominance rule applies in this instance any more than it did in the others.

Nevertheless, the effect of prefacing a discussion of individual self-mastery to the account of the city's self-discipline is undoubtedly to turn our thoughts towards externalization in this more than in any other instance. In order to explain the virtue of self-discipline in the city, Socrates first describes how, in the self-disciplined individual, a better part is in charge of a worse, then applies this description to the city. Here it turns out that what characterizes the better part - those who are best born and bred - is that one finds among them appetites that are governed by good sense, that is, by what in an individual would be his better part. It is hard to resist thinking that it is because self-disciplined individuals of the sort that Socrates first described are in control of the rest that the city turns out to resemble that sort of individual. It is easy to leap to the generalization that a city takes on the character of its rulers, and to read the correspondence between city and soul in its light.

Self-discipline, alone among the city's virtues, is explained by an analogy between soul and city, and the analogy runs in the opposite direction from that in which the city-soul correspondence otherwise operates. The correspondence in general takes an account of a virtue in the city and applies it to the individual. The account of self-discipline is in fact no exception; the corresponding virtue of the individual will later be derived, by analogy, from that of the city (442c-d). It is just that an additional account of the self-disciplined individual is inserted within that of the self-disciplined city, and here it is the city's virtue that is derived from the individual's virtue, not vice versa.

The later description of the self-disciplined individual, the one that derives from that of the self-disciplined city, takes up only one aspect of the city's virtue: the agreement between rulers and subjects as to who should rule. So within the self-disciplined soul spirit and appetite agree that reason should rule, and do not rebel against its authority. (True, the control of appetite by spirit and reason is described, but as an aspect of the soul's justice rather than of its self-discipline, 442a-b.) Glaucon chimes in at this point with an emphatic opinion: 'Yes. Self-discipline is nothing other than this (οὐκ ἄλλο τί ἐστιν ἢ τοῦτο), both for a city and for an individual' (442d). This serves to remind the reader that in fact self-discipline in the city was a couple of things other than this: it was the rule of superior over inferior (431b), and the control by the superior of the pleasures and desires found among the inferior (431c-d). These were just those aspects of the city's self-discipline that derived from the account of the self-disciplined individual inserted at that point. The idea that in this city rulers and subjects will be in agreement over who should rule is simply a claim that Socrates makes (431d). It makes good enough sense in light of his earlier descriptions of Callipolis; but it is not an idea that derives from his account of the self-disciplined individual. Rather, it is the idea from which his later definition of the self-disciplined individual will derive.

We are now in a position to appreciate why Plato imposed a detour through the virtue of the individual for this alone among the accounts of the city's virtues. In effect, he inserts an Isocratean pattern of analogy within his own, in order to put their differences on display. He inserts a derivation of the city's self-discipline from that of the individual, and adds the suggestion that it is because such individuals rule it that the city comes to be self-disciplined. This is a version of Isocrates' advice to King Nicocles. And the analytic emphasis falls as a result on differences in rank and on the control of inferior by superior, for only these are the features that emerge directly from the inserted comparison of individual and city. But when Socrates eventually derives the individual's virtue from the city's, following what will become his standard pattern, that person's self-discipline is modelled on the city's harmony and agreement, not on its adherence to rank or on the firmness of its control. That person is not looking to prove to himself that he is superior, like King Nicocles. Rather, he is keeping his soul quiet - the better, perhaps, to hear the divine voice within.

Notice that there is nothing inevitable about the results of these correspondences. It is not as if Socrates simply had to end up with a city distinguished for its divisions by rank and for the firmness of its control because he began his mapping with the individual, while conversely, when he projects from city to individual, he had to end up with an individual distinguished for his inner harmony rather than for a stiff upper lip. After all, his claim that the various classes in the city would agree over who should rule came quite out of the blue. Plato's script for the choices Socrates makes when explaining the correspondence of civic and individual self-discipline to Glaucon is written in such a way that it comments, for the reader, on Plato's own purposes when laying out the city-soul correspondence in general.

Self-discipline is in effect the favourite virtue of Glaucon and Adeimantus. True, they ask Socrates to come to the defence of justice; but their emphasis on its effects in the soul and their construal of justice as self-guardianship turns justice into a version of self-discipline, a care of the self. And they are just as interested in self-discipline on the civic scale. 'I wouldn't want it [the city's justice] to make its appearance too soon,' says Glaucon, 'if that means giving up the search for self-discipline. If I have any say in the matter, please examine self-discipline first (430d).' For Adeimantus' interest in the matter, consider the keenness of his distaste in Book 8 for loose behaviour in the democratic society, esp. 558a-c, 563a-e, and his unprompted claim that command over a city is the most difficult and important position of social responsibility that there is (χαλεπωτάτη καὶ μεγίστη ἡ ἀρχή, 551c).

Socrates, by contrast, is reluctant to address the topic, and for the very same reason that Glaucon is eager. Glaucon's enthusiasm suggests that of Isocrates' ideal ruler, ambitious to earn by personal self-discipline the right to impose discipline on his society. We saw in chapter 1 that the brothers, in their quietism, retreat from rather than rise above political ambition; and we have seen in the previous chapter that they are only too happy to identify themselves with the rulers of Callipolis, and how this could block their appreciation of what Callipolis can reveal as analogue for the individual. In contrast to Glaucon's eagerness to examine civic self-discipline, Socrates' reluctance resembles that of Plato's philosopher-king, who submits to rather than welcomes the dual necessity of ordering the inferior elements of his society and those of his own soul.

Within the frame of this reluctance, Socrates' account of the city's self-discipline is free to match the *hauteur* that we have seen Glaucon and Adeimantus exhibit. In chapter 2 I attempted to disarm Williams' protests on behalf of the unjustly maligned workers of Callipolis, and showed that the music of the city's self-discipline seems intended to have warmth and appeal. Only a dull ear, however, could be deaf to the tone of a comment such as this:

> But you do also find a whole range and variety of desires, pleasures, and pains. Particularly in children, women, slaves, and among so-called free men, in the majority of ordinary people (ἐν παισὶ

μάλιστα ἄν τις εὕροι καὶ γυναιξὶ καὶ οἰκέταις καὶ τῶν ἐλευθέρων λεγομένων ἐν τοῖς πολλοῖς τε καὶ φαύλοις). (431b-c)

But it is to such passages that we should look for the source of Socrates' reluctance. The control of inferior elements in the healthy soul and in the healthy society has no magic for him as it has for Glaucon.

2. The tyrant

Isocrates' advice to King Nicocles is externalization at its noblest, but it remains mired in the middle ground on which the individual moves in society. It makes an analogy between soul and city but does not pluck the fruit that such an analogy offers: the conjoint yet distinct awareness of little and big - of individual microcosm and political macrocosm. If you try to link little with big by externalizing the one onto the other - whether theoretically, by assuming that a society derives its character from rulers of analogous character who have shaped it in their image, or practically, by entering government and attempting to externalize yourself onto your society - you will lose the possibility of this awareness. The two instances in which the *Republic* shows an individual actually governing a society of analogous character are adapted, in their different ways, to illustrate this point. Although Callipolis is indeed an image of the philosopher that rules it, the philosopher has not sought to make it in his image. He rules Callipolis with just the awareness of little and big recommended by the city-soul analogy. At the other extreme is the person of tyrannical character who gets to become an actual tyrant. He represents externalization at its worst - at its furthest from the awareness of microcosm and macrocosm.

Let us take that worst case first. Because a tyranny is, by definition, the rule of a single man, Socrates' account of the tyrannical society in Book 8 includes a description of the individual tyrant who comes to hold power in it. So the question arises, more pressingly than it did for the other cities and corresponding souls: Does this actual tyrant have the character of the tyrannical individual described in Book 9 - the individual whose soul is analogous in its elements and structure to the tyrannical society? It is quite clear that, conversely, a tyrannical character need not be an actual tyrant, for in Book 9 Socrates attributes that character to an assortment of low-lifes, including those who serve as an actual tyrant's bodyguard (575b-c). But it becomes equally clear in Book 9 that the reigning tyrant described in Book 8 is to be thought of as a tyrannical character.

Socrates explains that if there are a large enough number of tyrannical men in the city, they will take advantage of the folly of the populace and transform one such man into 'that tyrant' (τὸν τύραννον γεννῶντες... ἐκεῖνον, 575c) - that is, the tyrant whose rise was described in Book 8. They will select whichever of them has the 'biggest and most bloated tyrant in his soul' (μέγιστον καὶ πλεῖστον ἐν τῇ ψυχῇ τύραννον ἔχει). But this event takes place outside the terms of the analogy. In Book 8 we read how the people, led by dronish demagogues, would bring the tyrant into being as their champion (γεννήσας, 568e; cf. 565c). What this corresponds to in the soul, however, is the installation of lust as champion of the idle desires that consume whatever is available (573a). That is, Socrates has already explained the correspondence between tyranny and the tyrannical man, and the connection that he now suggests between having the greatest tyrant in one's soul and being qualified to become the greatest tyrant of one's city is not required in order to fill out the terms of that correspondence. It is an additional point.

This is not to deny that the point draws its strength from the analogy between tyranny and the tyrannical man. But the reason this is so is not that the city-soul analogy in general follows an externalization rule, but that both tyranny and the tyrannical man have a special bond with the phenomenon of externalization.

Having described how democracy degenerates into tyranny through the tyrant's rise to power as champion of the people, Socrates launches his account of civic life under a tyranny in Book 8 with these words:

> Shall we then describe the happiness of this man and of the city (τοῦ τε ἀνδρὸς καὶ τῆς πόλεως) where such a creature comes into being? (566d)

We are to consider the condition of a city and of a man, but not as we have been doing so far in Book 8, considering first a city and then the man whose soul is structured analogously. A tyranny is distinct among other cities for being a mere extension of the interests of a single man, its tyrant. We cannot consider its civic life as a whole, as we have that of timocracy, oligarchy, and democracy, but must think of it as the life of one distinct star supported by a civic nebula.

The tyrant has a natural propensity to reduce his city to an expression of his individual will, for only so can he maintain absolute power. He wants no peers, brooks no independence in others; he leads his city into unnecessary wars for purely selfish reasons, in order to reinforce his personal

95

supremacy (566e-567c). Eventually, with the aid of mercenary henchmen, he reduces his citizens to the condition of personal slaves (568d-569c). If the city in which these wretched slaves reside itself glitters and is glorious, that glory and glitter belong personally to the tyrant. (Syracuse under Dionysius I was noted for its splendour and was, in externals, a great city.) It is he, the tyrant, who wins the city's wars. He must, or he would lose his throne. It is the tyrant, not his city, who attracts and commissions poets and dramatists from abroad. These artists will deliver at court rather than at public festivals, where they will praise not his city, but him (568a-d).

In short, the tyrant represents the ambition to externalize oneself at its most shameless. If the Isocratean pattern makes the mistake of attempting to externalize the little letters onto the big, it does at least resolve the words into their letters, pay due regard to the fact that both man and city are structures of parts, microcosm and macrocosm. The tyrant, however, acts as an atom. He pays no regard either to his own internal processes or to those of his city, but externalizes his will as something indivisible. When the city acts, it will be as if the tyrant has acted; the city will act not as a whole but as an individual. It will go into war with other cities and this war will be the tyrant's personal campaign, while internal civic tensions are either ignored or ruthlessly quashed. Its grand buildings and boulevards, its roster of artists will dazzle, but as peacock feathers in the tyrant's cap, while all beauty fades from the lives of its citizens.

Consider now the analogous process in the soul of the tyrannical man. As the tyrant ends up reducing the city to an extension of himself, causing the city to act among other cities as if it were the tyrant incarnate, so the tyrannical man's inner tyrant, his 'passion' or 'lust' (ἔρως), does not stop when it has taken control of the entire soul (573d) and rejected older and milder pleasures in favour of more violent ones (574a). It proceeds to turn the entire person into an extension of itself, causing him to act among other people as if he were that passion incarnate. So the tyrannical man will come to blows with his older, milder parents and make them serve the drunken pals he has brought home (574a-c). As the tyrant led his city into wars that benefited only him, so the tyrannical man's inner tyrant will lead him 'like a city' (ὥσπερ πόλιν, 575a) to commit crimes that will subsidize only its own extravagant needs. That inner tyrant has broken out of the confines of the soul and entered the world of men; the tyrannical man has become in waking life something that at an earlier stage of his degeneration lived only in his dreams (574e).

This portrait of the tyrannical man is based on analogical reasoning. But due to the distinctive features of the model on which it is based - due to this, not due to the standard mechanism of the city-soul analogy - the result is a character whom it is natural to connect not just analogically but causally with the corresponding city. For there is no reason why the tyrannical man's inner tyrant should be content to lord it over a household and commit petty crime, once it has broken out into the world of men. There is every reason why it should be ambitious for the big time and try to lord it over an entire city, if it gets the chance; why, as Socrates says, enslaving not just mother or father but motherland or fatherland should 'be the ultimate goal at which the tyrannical man's desire is directed' (τέλος ἂν εἴη τῆς ἐπιθυμίας τοῦ τοιούτου ἀνδρός, 575d).

We may assume, then, that Adeimantus' comment on the idea that the people's champion in Book 8 will be chosen for having the biggest tyrant in his soul is quite as exact and revealing as those comparable comments we have seen him interpose about unsound individuals who correspond to their cities. 'Very probably. After all, he would be the most tyrannical' (Εἰκότως γ', ἔφη· τυραννικώτατος γὰρ ἂν εἴη, 575d). That an actual tyrant will be a tyrannical man is a likelihood, no more and no less. The people will tend to choose that man among them who will make the most voracious and unscrupulous wolf when it comes to wresting power and resources from the wealthy (565c-566a), forgetting that such a man will not stop with destroying the rich. And it is likely that the one who stands out as the most voracious wolf will be the man with a passion for total power over others and a propensity for violence - the tyrannical man.

This likelihood is grounded in human nature, not in the city-soul analogy. What the analogy will proceed to show is that, if we look into the soul of this wolf who lords it so magnificently over the trembling sheep, on the assumption that this wolf has the character of a tyrannical man, we will find that his soul trembles no less wretchedly than do those sheep. Projecting the democratic man's way of life onto the big screen of a democracy permitted us, we found, to penetrate its apparent ease and freedom and discern its anarchy and chaos. Likewise, projecting the tyrannical man's way of life onto the big screen of a tyranny penetrates what might seem enviable in it - the power to push others around - and reveals it as enslavement (577d-e). But this time there is a twist to the argument: the tyrannical man in whom we are especially interested is the one who becomes an actual tyrant. The way of life that the analogy penetrates is the one most in need of penetration, because most likely to dazzle with its outward show, with the 'theatrical costume and props' (τραγικὴ σκευή) of the tyrant's court (577a-b). And by this twist to the argument Plato adds a more exquisite pain to his dagger-thrust in the tyrant's heart. It emerges that if anything can make yet more wretched the inner life of a tyrannical man, it is that boost to his worst drives, that extra scope for friendlessness and insatiability afforded by his becoming an actual tyrant and strutting a global stage (578c-580a).

The tyrannical man is, we may say, a natural externalizer. But we must distinguish the externalization that he *thinks* is going on from what is actually happening. He imagines that he is turning those around him into an extension of his personal will, beginning with his household and extending the circle as wide as opportunity permits. This we understand when we look back on the portrait of the man who becomes tyrant in Book 8 having learnt in Book 9 to see him not only as a tyrant but as tyrannical. What his ambition to externalize himself is really doing to him, the match between inside and outside that is actually being made: this escapes his notice. But he will certainly experience its results.

The tyrannical man does not set out to enslave himself; but inevitably, it is what he ends up doing. That would be why there is repeated mention of the 'mischance' or 'misfortune' that 'compels' a tyrannical man to become a tyrant (ὑπὸ τινὸς συμφορᾶς, 578c; ἀναγκασθῇ ὑπὸ τινὸς τύχης, 579c). If he knew what he was doing to himself, this is how he would regard fortune's offer. His ambition, if he knew what he was doing to himself, would stand revealed as a twisted version of Isocrates' counsel to King Nicocles. Not: Rule yourself, so that you may be qualified to rule others. Rather: Tyrannize yourself, so that you may be qualified to tyrannize others.

By refusing to be dazzled by the tyrant's external show, and by attending to how the city-soul analogy penetrates it, we can deflect the objection that a psychological wreck like the tyrannical man would lack the steely determination necessary to hold power in the teeth of his enemies, as well as the connected objection that the profiles of many actual tyrants conform closely to the steely stereotype. This would include the most famous tyrant of Plato's day, and the one he is assumed to have in mind in Book 9: Dionysius I. (These are Julia Annas' objections.)[12]

For Plato does not deny that a reigning tyrant will be an accomplished and formidable wolf. When he compares such a tyrant to a physically sick, weak man who attempts to fight those with better physiques (579c), he is not referring to the tyrant's outer life, his ability to despatch rivals and maintain his grip on power. The argument is that for all his wolfish exterior, and no matter if he died in his bed, even Dionysius I was self-tyrannized. A weakling cannot successfully fight strong opponents; likewise, Dionysius - despite his success as a tyrant - was a failure as a ruler. All his life, we may suppose, he recognized that he was surrounded in the Greek world by his civic and spiritual superiors. This was a battle he fought and lost, and knew himself to have lost. One thinks here of his sad attempts to gain respect not only as a patron of poets but as a poet himself.

Let us note, finally, that no departure is required from the regular pattern of analogical argument in order to demonstrate the tyrannical man's wretchedness. Norbert Blössner points out that a tyranny is more exactly a tyrannized society having a tyrant as its tyrannizer; and he accuses Plato of identifying the tyrannical man exclusively with the oppressed populace, an identification from which his unhappiness follows all too easily. This Blössner contrasts with the earlier pattern of comparing the individual man exclusively with the ruling class of the city to which he corresponds.[13]

Ample evidence has shown, I trust, that there is no such earlier pattern. In each instance, the individual is compared to the corresponding city as a whole, not to any particular class within it. But it is equally clear that the correspondence of tyrannical man and tyranny is no exception to this rule. At one point, Socrates challenges Glaucon's confidence that the tyrannized city is enslaved rather than free with the consideration that it contains masters and free men. Glaucon replies:

[12] Annas 1981, 304.
[13] Blössner 1997, 163.

I can see a small element of that. Not much. But more or less the whole thing (τὸ δὲ ὅλον, ὡς ἔπος εἰπεῖν) - and certainly the most decent element in it - is shamefully and miserably enslaved. (577c)

The comparison with the tyrannical man sweeps all of these elements in its view. His soul is almost entirely enslaved, with only a tiny part of himself holding sway, and that the worst and most insane (577d). The man as a whole is compared to the city as a whole, and no attempt is made to conceal that some small part of him gets to do exactly as it pleases, and tyrannize the rest.

But why should a tyrannical man care, we might wonder, about the parts of himself that he has enslaved and allowed to atrophy? That 'tiny' part which has its way provides him, after all, with big pleasures. He loves to push people around, and he is spending his days doing what he loves. He does not care, he might tell us, that he loves no other human being and is loved by none; does not care that he has no true friends, only allies against his enemies. *Oderint, dum metuant.* He lives always on the edge, 'forever driven on by the gadfly of desire (οἴστρου)' (577e); but what if the edge is just where he wants to be?

It seems we must already be disposed to see ourselves as microcosms, as the city-soul analogy recommends, in order to find convincing the account of the tyrannical man's unhappiness that is the outcome of this analogy. To the extent that we believe no part of our make-up can be neglected or abused with impunity - and it is the philosopher-king who puts this belief into practice most completely - we will want to perceive the tyrannical man's defiance as bluster, perhaps desperate bluster. It took a Glaucon, an Adeimantus to ask what justice and injustice do to our souls. The question never even occurred to Thrasymachus.

3. The philosopher-king

If the tyrannical man who comes into a tyranny stands for externalization at its worst, and if the Isocratean model is externalization at its noblest, the philosopher in Callipolis stands for something beyond externalization and better than it. His relation to Callipolis is not the star example of externalization that Jonathan Lear would have it be. Rather, the philosopher-king puts into practice the awareness of little and big conveyed for the reader of the *Republic* by the city-soul analogy. Externalization plays no part in that analogy; nor does it in the practice of the philosopher-king.

100

It is certainly true that in Callipolis what we have been calling the pre-dominance rule applies. Callipolis is ruled by those whose souls are structured analogously to the civic order over which they preside (498e, 590d). But this is neither a consequence of how the city-soul analogy standardly works, nor of any externalizing ambition in the philosopher. It is a result demanded by the laws of Callipolis, as established by its 'founders' (519c) - Socrates and his discussion partners. The tyrannical man becomes a tyrant because, we saw, some chance compels him to the throne; and this compulsion reflects the disparity between his intentions and their realization. He seeks to tyrannize his city but in doing so is himself internally tyrannized; a match is effected be-tween himself and his city that he did not plan and that gives him no delight.

That a kind of compulsion is likewise imposed on philosophers in order to make them kings is thematic in the *Republic,* and the theme even ap-pears once in association with chance, as it did for the tyrant: our hope must be, says Socrates in Book 6, that existing philosophers are 'compelled by some chance event (ἀνάγκη τις ἐκ τύχης περιβάλῃ), whether they like it or not, to take charge of their city' (499b). It is not that the philosopher is unwilling to take up the burden of rule, in the sense that he would avoid doing so if he could; this we saw in chapter 1. But the theme of compulsion accurately expresses how he too has a match effected for him between his soul and his city that was not of his planning. It is the law that makes this match. There is even a sense in which the match gives him no delight: not that he suffers inner torment as does the reigning tyrant; but he cannot glory in kingship, cannot find it 'fine' or 'beautiful', καλόν (540b).

The law matches the philosopher's soul to his city, but that is not its goal. Its goal is to make the whole city flourish (519e), and for this it is necessary to raise to power those who can fashion the city after the pattern of justice and rational order that holds among the forms, the eternal objects of knowledge (484c-d, 500d, 501a-c). Those people are the philosophers, whom contemplative association with that rational order has prompted to assimilate themselves to its pattern (500c). Philosophers have internalized the pattern of the forms; it has become a pattern or model in their souls to guide their actions (484c). Thus, when the rulers of Callipolis regulate their city, they do so according to a pattern that is also found in their own souls. But here is the crucial point: it is not to their own souls that the rulers of Cal-lipolis look when they regulate their city. They look to the forms directly, and regulate the city after that pattern, just as they look to that pattern to regulate their own souls (484c, 500d, 501b). No externalization is involved.

Philosophers do not serve up to the city the rational order of the forms that they have cooked in their souls. The twin procedures of regulating one-self and one's city are lifelong and go on at the same remove from the forms; philosopher-kings will perform each in turn (540a-b).

To say that the regulation of self and city proceed at the same remove from the forms is not to say that they are related to the forms in exactly the same way. The philosopher who puts his city in order is described as a painter taking the city as his canvas and the forms as his model (484c, 501a-b); but the imitative process by which a philosopher comes to assimilate himself personally to the forms is less deliberate and seems more a consequence of loving association (500c). (The formulation at 540a is broad enough to cover both types of imitation.) The contrast reflects the difference in the types of constraint that bind the philosopher to himself and to the city he rules. The city is artificial, a creation of human beings; the philosopher, as a human being, is a natural creature. He is bound up with his 'inner constitution' (τὴν ἐν αὐτῷ πολιτείαν, 591e) with a bond more inescapable than that which ties him to Callipolis, where the force of law is required to supplement that of nature.

Still, the philosopher's way of dealing with self-regulation and regulation of the city is in both cases to imitate the forms. And whatever exactly this involves, it certainly entails looking outside of oneself and of the city. As a result, when the philosopher looks back at self and at city, he sees each from the outside, as self-contained wholes. This is what permits him to see the one as microcosm and the other as macrocosm. He does not, as everyone else does, prefer to determine a man's value by what he can make of himself in society, nor the value of a society by what it can do for a particular individual or interest group.

Certainly, living in Callipolis is best for the philosopher personally as well as for the city as a whole. In a political system which is worthy of him, says Socrates, the philosopher's 'own growth will be greater (αὐτός τε μᾶλλον αὐξήσεται), and he will be the salvation of his country as well as himself' (497a). By comparison with the philosopher who must spend his life sheltered behind a wall of purity from a city in turmoil, his achievement is the 'greatest' (μέγιστα) that a philosopher can achieve before his departure from human life. But that is a crucial qualification; it is what distinguishes Socrates' claim from Isocrates' urging King Nicocles to think of kingship as the 'greatest' of human activities. It is best for the philosopher personally to live in a city that supports philosophers and their activity. It is philosophy that is the greatest of human activities. And it produces the kind of person whose reason for consenting to regulate a city that supports philosophers is not just that this is best for him personally, but that it is best for the city as a whole.

By raising to power in Callipolis the man who resembles Callipolis, the argument achieves a twist comparable to its treatment of the tyrannical man who becomes a tyrant. The fulfilment of that man's ambition to gain a tyranny turned out to be the one thing that could make his own condition yet more miserable; so the philosopher's acceding to power turns out, equally unexpectedly, to be the one thing that can make his own condition yet finer. It is equally unexpected, but not for the reason that applies to the tyrant. In the tyrant's case it is odd, or at least ironic, that the fulfilment of a person's ambition should turn out to be his ruin. But the benefit the philosopher derives from power is unexpected just because power was never his ambition.

This contrast is reflected in the phrasing that Socrates gives to the final verdict in Book 9 (580c) on the relative happiness and unhappiness of the two men. The happiest man is 'the most kingly, the one who is king over himself' (τὸν βασιλικώτατον καὶ βασιλεύοντα αὑτοῦ), while the most wretched is 'the one with the most tyrannical nature, the one who is the greatest tyrant over himself and his city' (τυραννικώτατος ὢν ἑαυτοῦ τε ὅτι μάλιστα τυραννῇ καὶ τῆς πόλεως). Whereas the description of the tyrannical man fits the Isocratean pattern and externalizes his inner condition onto that of his city, the description of the best and most just man, the philosopher, mentions only his rule over himself and leaves his rule over others implicit in the word βασιλικώτατος, 'most kingly'.

Not only is the word by itself a solemn and resonant superlative; this is also its only occurrence anywhere in Plato's dialogues. So it seems quite likely that Plato is using it to mark his position off from those who used the term in the more limited way that he transcends in the *Republic*: notably Isocrates, whom we saw urging King Nicocles to consider 'most kingly' the ability to control oneself no less than one controls the citizenry, but also perhaps Xenophon, who describes the Persian king Cyrus as βασιλικώτατός τε καὶ ἄρχειν ἀξιώτατος, 'most kingly, and most worthy to rule' (*Anabasis* 1.9.1). Of the two, it was Isocrates who was provoked to react. In the *Areopagiticus* (14), written in the last decade of Plato's life, and again in the *Panathenaicus*

(138), written after Plato's death, Isocrates writes that a city's constitution (πολιτεία) is its soul (ψυχή), and 'has the same power as intelligence has in the body' (τοσαύτην ἔχουσα δύναμιν ὅσην περ ἐν σώματι φρόνησις), for it is thoughtful about the common good.

The type of metaphor or simile that Plato so carefully skirted, in which an element of the city is described as an element of the soul, a type that is the converse of one that Isocrates had himself used earlier, now appears for the first time in Isocrates' work - and more explicitly than in any political writer of the time, not excepting Aristotle *Politics* 4.9.3 [1294a39-95b1]. It may be a defiant appearance - a flaunting of what Plato refused to write - or the words may have been written in new-found sympathy with the rather different position Plato takes in the *Laws;* for the city's intelligence in Isocrates' formulation is not its ruling class but its constitution. Notice also how Isocrates' thought in *Areopagiticus* 14 concludes. Both politicians and private individuals will inevitably conform or 'assimilate themselves' (ὁμοιοῦσθαι) to the constitution, and their actions will proceed accordingly. That almost automatic process of assimilation which in the *Republic* takes place between philosophers and the forms, here takes place between all citizens, expert and non-expert, and the constitution of their city. It is hard not to believe that Isocrates recognized in the city-soul analogy of the *Republic* a critique directed at his views on kingship, and here offers a response.

But at one point the *Republic* too speaks of assimilating oneself to the constitution of Callipolis rather than to the forms on which that constitution was based. At the very end of Book 9 (592b) Socrates mentions the unlikelihood that the just man will ever be able to enter government in his own country, then insists that whether or not Callipolis exists anywhere or ever will, it is the only city such a man would have anything to do with. For there is perhaps 'a model laid up in the heavens' (ἐν οὐρανῷ... παράδειγμα) for anyone who chooses to see it, and that person can proceed to 'found a city within himself' (ἑαυτὸν κατοικίζειν) on the basis of what he has seen.

Myles Burnyeat, to whom is due the translation 'in the heavens' rather than the more traditional 'in heaven', compares *Timaeus* 47c and suggests that the model in question is literally to be observed in the sky above. Here as in the *Timaeus,* he claims, 'what the philosopher's intellect will assimilate... is the orderly circular motions that drive the heavenly bodies.'[14] But for one thing, Timaeus is explaining the greatest good derivable from the use of the eyes (47b), not the greatest good derivable from the use of the intellect; and for another, the suggestion is hard to square with the subordinate status of astronomy as a component of the philosopher's training in the *Republic.*

If it is correct to insist on an astronomical reference for the 'model in the heavens', that reference should direct the reader in the first instance not to the *Timaeus* but to the *Republic*'s recommendation to imagine that the patterns formed by the heavenly bodies are diagrams drawn by Daedalus or some such master draughtsman, and thus to treat them as 'models' (παραδείγμασι, 529d) through which to understand the true numbers and motions that drive those bodies. The model in the heavens that is Callipolis is not astronomical, but like the heavenly bodies it is to be imagined as a picture or diagram drawn by a master draughtsman - not Daedalus, however, but Plato.

Glaucon supposes that if Callipolis is to be found nowhere on earth then we must call it a 'city in words' (τῇ ἐν λόγοις κειμένῃ, 592a). What does Socrates' calling it a city in the sky add to Glaucon's idea? Callipolis is not a form - it does not have the status of the true motions that drive the heavenly bodies (Callipolis is not a mathematical, either, if that and not a form is what a true motion is.) Callipolis is like the stars in being a beautiful model that reveals the equivalent of true motions - the true virtues by which it is structured.

There are two ways in which you can use the stars as a model. By treating them as the finest, most beautiful (κάλλιστα, 529c, e) creation of their type, you can learn something about the true motions and numbers from which their beauty ultimately derives. This is what Socrates recommends in Book 7 (μαθήσεως ἕνεκα, 529d). Equally, you could use observation of the heavens as a spiritual exercise that brings order to the motions of your

[14] Burnyeat 2001; compare Burnyeat 1992, 177.

own soul, which come to be like those of the stars and planets. This seems to be what the *Timaeus* recommends. Whether the two ways are in fact one would depend on the degree of conscious purpose we attribute to the philosopher's assimilation to the forms described at 500c. The correct study of astronomy might brings its spiritual benefits more or less automatically. The *Timaeus,* however, speaks of 'using' the movements of the stars to produce an effect on the orbits of the mind (χρησαίμεθα ἐπί..., 47b).

Be that as it may, the answer to our question is that by raising Callipolis to the sky Socrates suggests that it too, like the stars, should be treated as the most beautiful imaginable creation of its type - the type that consists of human artefacts. For Callipolis is a creation, Plato's creation, whether or not it ever gets built somewhere. The craftsman who built the heavens was a god. Once he set his mind to creating the most beautiful embodiment of true number and true motions, the thing got built. But Plato is only human; the most beautiful city he can build is in a book.

Suppose you painted a picture, suggests Socrates in Book 5, that could serve as a model of the most beautiful man imaginable (παράδειγμα οἷον ἂν εἴη ὁ κάλλιστος ἄνθρωπος, 472d): would you be any the worse a painter if you could not demonstrate that such a man could ever exist? Socrates is tempering Glaucon's eagerness to know how Callipolis could be made real. For it is the Callipolis portrayed in Plato's book, not the Callipolis that might one day just possibly get built, that is the equivalent of the model man, the beautiful man in the painting, and comes closest to the beautiful model in the heavens. No society made up of living human beings, not even if it is Callipolis, can equal the embodied beauty of the heavens, for what is created mortal cannot match what is created divine (*Timaeus* 34b, 41a-d).

A book can come closer to this ideal. Not only are words more malleable than wax and free from the constraints of practicality (473a, 588d), but books can live longer than any city - a truth borne out not least by the fate of the *Republic.* And if we cannot live in a book, still the *Republic* is creation enough, embodiment enough, to be a model for each of us to take within our souls rather as the astronomer assimilates what is too far off for him to reach.

Indeed, it is a good deal easier for an individual to embody this model some place, some time, than it would be for him to get Callipolis built. When it comes to our individual lives, each of us can be something like the craftsman god who made the stars. If we set our minds to it, and if those minds are good enough, the thing will get built. This is not to say that human lives are man-made artefacts like human cities; for human beings are divine creations, even though god created humans to have responsibility for running their individual lives, not only their cities (617e). Callipolis remains the most beautiful human artefact, then, despite the fact that a man is something more, and more beautiful, than a city.

Socrates' parting words in Book 9 are not said with philosopher-kings in mind but amount to a recommendation directed by Plato at his readers. Gazing at the model of Callipolis is not something the philosopher-king will do. He will not read books about Callipolis but live and govern there; he will gaze at the forms and apply his understanding of them to the benefit of his city, as Plato gazed at the forms in order to imagine that city. The reader's understanding of these matters comes by comparison at second-hand, although it may stimulate him to some original thinking - may direct his gaze towards the forms.

Plato is not, however, suggesting that the reader who does nothing but *think* about Callipolis should feel completely satisfied with himself. When Socrates says of the model city in the sky that 'it makes no difference whether it exists anywhere, or ever will' (592b), he does not mean that this makes no difference at all; he means that the model remains as useful either way for the purpose he has just ascribed to one who chooses to gaze upon it and 'found a city within himself' (ἑαυτὸν κατοικίζειν, 592b). After all, he does not elaborate this claim with some such thought as 'Building the thing, you see, is an ambition for small minds', but offers rather the explanation (γὰρ) that 'It, and no other, is the only city he would have anything to do with.' That is, one can cleave to this resolve whether or not the city ever exists.

If Plato is not recommending that we need do no more than think about Callipolis, that is because it remains true that the 'greatest' (μέγιστον) achievement is for the philosopher to find a political system worthy of him, where 'his own growth will be greater and he can be the salvation of his country as well as of himself' (497a). This remains the greatest human achievement, but is not the 'most beautiful' (κάλλιστον). Only when a god is the craftsman can the greatest creation also be the most beautiful. And as we know, the philosopher will not find the task of ruling 'beautiful' at all (καλόν, 540b).

Still, why would the philosopher be anything but enthusiastic about building Callipolis, one might think, if his own growth will be greater there? Notice first that if it makes no difference to the task of founding a city within oneself whether Callipolis exists or not, then it cannot be the philosopher's inner condition that becomes yet finer when he 'grows'. One can perfect the inner 'regime' (πολιτεία), live a blameless life (496d-e), while living under any regime (496d-e, 591e). But it is as with Themistocles' rebuttal of the man from Seriphus (329e). When the Seriphian complained that it was Themistocles' city, not his own efforts, that had made him famous, 'Themistocles' reply was that though he himself would never have been famous if he had been born in Seriphus, neither would the other man have been if he had been born in Athens.' A nice reply, but it cost Themistocles the admission that no man can stretch himself to greatness in a narrow place.

The philosopher too, if he should fall as a seed in the soil of Callipolis (497c), will 'become a greater man' (μᾶλλον αὐξήσει, 497a). A greater man, not a better one; at least, not better than those who manage to escape being spoiled by falling as seed in inappropriate soil (496b-c, 497b). But whereas their divine nature is kept behind walls, where they take shelter from the civic storm (496d), his will be allowed to 'shine' (δηλώσει, 497c).

The philosophers in Callipolis are given the means to do good for their society, and, being good, they take the opportunity to do it. They also feel that they owe this as τροφεῖα, a debt incurred by upbringing, to the city that sponsored their philosophic development (520b-e). But Plato's philosophic achievement is rather the 'spontaneous growth' that he contrasts with theirs; it developed despite his city, not with its blessing (520a). It is reasonable, says Socrates, for such a man not to take part in politics, nor to be eager to repay a debt that was never incurred (520b). If Plato were to take the opportunity to do good in the political realm, he would be doing so because he is good, and wants the good to be effective; and doubtless he would also have no objection to becoming great. If he were nevertheless not to seek out this opportunity, but concentrate his efforts instead on writing the *Republic,* that would be because the greatest achievement for human beings is not the most beautiful.

For philosophers in Callipolis the question of not seeking out such an opportunity does not arise. They are raised for this task; the opportunity is guaranteed by law. But in the *Seventh Letter* Dion ascribes to 'divine fortune' (θεία τινὶ τύχῃ) the opportunity to turn the Sicilian monarch into a philosopher (327e). It is an opportunity that Plato had not foreseen but, he writes, could not refuse, not when so much good could result; not when refusal would incur the 'greatest' (μέγιστον) charge, the charge that he was unwilling to take on the burden of deeds but was a man of words alone (those most beautiful words...); not when he owed this, if not as τροφεῖα to the city of Syracuse, then as a debt of friendship to Dion, the actual creator of this supposedly heaven-sent opportunity (328c-d).

With Socrates' parting note at the end of Book 9, Plato suggests that the first step towards building our little cosmos is to gaze at Callipolis and understand how a human being can be like it. Let that first step be the last taken in this book. Perhaps surprisingly, it is not a step taken in the *Republic* itself. But it is a step the *Republic* explicitly prepares its readers to take.

4. The city and man

When in Book 4 Socrates prepares to apply the analogue of the virtuous city to the soul of the virtuous individual, he issues a caveat:

> Now let us apply our findings there to the individual. If they agree, well and good. If we come to some other conclusion about the individual, then we shall go back to the city again, and test it on that. If we look at the two side by side, perhaps we can get a spark from them. Like rubbing dry sticks together. If that makes justice appear, we shall have confirmed it to our satisfaction. (434e-435a)

The findings proceed in Book 4 to agree at least to Glaucon's satisfaction; for when justice turns out to be health of the soul he is ready to bring the argument to a close. But we saw that Socrates is not. He insists on filling out the analogy between the unsound cities and individuals, and before he can do so is diverted into filling out the details of life in Callipolis (Books 5-7). The result is that a rather different individual turns out to be the best imaginable: not simply a man of healthy soul, but the philosopher who both rules in and resembles Callipolis. As Glaucon says in Book 8, looking back on Books 5-7: 'You apparently had an even better city and individual to tell us about' (543d).

The philosopher too has a healthy soul, of course. But true virtue does not end for him in health of the soul - this we saw in chapter 1. The reasoning element in him is directed at something greater and more godlike than the inner politics that is its concern in Book 4, even if inner politics remains one of its concerns. The philosopher takes care of his soul out of a sense of necessity, compelled by his humanity. But a kind of necessity was among the most distinctive factors added to the constitution of Callipolis; philosophers are compelled to become its kings. There is a fresh correspondence to be drawn, then, between the completely virtuous city and the completely virtuous man.

Socrates prefaces his account of the analogy between unsound cities and individuals with the claim that 'we have finished describing the person who resembles aristocracy (τὸν μὲν δὴ ἀριστοκρατίᾳ ὅμοιον διεληλύθαμεν ἤδη). And we say, quite rightly, that he is good and just' (544e). This is true enough of the person described in Book 4; less true of the philosopher. His character has been described in Books 5-6, and it has been made clear that the philosopher-king is the just man ruling in the just city (498e). But there has been no formal elaboration of the correspondence between Callipolis and the philosopher in the manner of Books 4 and 8.

Socrates mentions, in fact, that he is leaving the job undone. Here is the close of Book 7:

> 'Isn't our discussion of this city, and the corresponding individual, now complete? After all, I imagine it's pretty clear what we are going to say that individual should be like (δῆλος γάρ που καὶ οὗτος οἷον φήσομεν αὐτὸν εἶναι).'
> 'Yes, it is clear,' he said. 'And in reply to your question, I do think this subject of discussion is complete'. (541b)

It is indeed pretty clear what we will say he should be like. It is certainly clear enough for Glaucon, smitten as he has been by the magnificence of the philosopher-king. But that does not mean there is nothing to more to say about how the man resembles the city. Elaborating that correspondence may be how Plato intended us to kindle the spark in our souls, that spark from firesticks which in the *Seventh Letter* (341c, 344b) is the image for the result of an individual's long association with a matter of importance to him.

To see how this correspondence would differ from that between the just city and the just man described in Book 4 - prior to Socrates' injecting the philosopher-king into his argument - we should begin from those features that distinguish the city described in Books 5-7. Most obviously, it is ruled by philosophers. Also, those philosophers rule only because they recognize that this is necessary, not out of ambition. This was not brought out in the earlier books, when only guardians, not philosopher-kings, were in view. Socrates' concern with the guardians was not in getting them to see the necessity of their rule, but with ensuring that their dog-like agression should not turn wolfish and be reversed against their fellow-citizens.

In Callipolis, the typical relation between absolute rulers and their subjects in the ancient world is reversed. Its citizens willingly subject themselves to their rulers, whom they regard as saviours (463a-b), even though this cooperation is initially achieved by the expulsion of all but the children - which is to say, of all who are likely to prove unmalleable. In order for the philosopher-kings to be vaulted into power, on the other hand, we have seen that some 'necessity' is imagined to 'happen upon them', compelling them to take charge of a city 'whether they like it or not' (499b).

A final distinctive feature: the level of military discipline imposed on the auxiliaries - the class from which the philosopher-kings of Callipolis are chosen - turns out in Book 5 to exceed anything even Sparta could exhibit. Domestic life in separate families is to be abolished; women will fight in the army and be freed from the duties of childrearing; the military class will be one huge family, kept unaware of their blood-line by the secret manipulations of the philosopher-kings, who will manage them as if breeding for quality from a herd of animals. By these measures the army will achieve unparalleled unity and *esprit de corps,* and become unquestioningly loyal, ready to sacrifice their personal interest, upon command, for the city's sake (462a-e, 464a-b).

What would the soul that corresponds to such a regime look like? The role of the ruling class in the best city, we remember, corresponds to that of reason in the soul of the best individual; the role of the military class is taken by spirit; while the role of the subject citizenry, the yeomen and craftsmen, corresponds to that of materialistic desires. Let us see what results.

Take first the relation between reason and spirit. The unity and loyalty of the military class is achieved by deceptive manipulation on the part of the rulers for the benefit of those they rule (459b-c). And it turns out that, when Socrates warned his audience how accomplished and daring these rulers would have to be to succeed at such a task (459b), he had in mind that philosophers alone were up to it. They alone would have a full grasp of the principles on which the city is organized, the same grasp as that of its founders, the participants in this discussion (473e, 497c-d). Philosophers, however, form a class quite distinct from the regular military. In this they differ from the rulers described in Book 3 (412c-e), who were simply those senior members of the military who had shown themselves most able and self-sacrificing. In other words, only through the agency of philosophers do the soldiers become a distinct, unitary class of auxiliaries.

This corresponds exactly with a development in the analysis of the just individual as between Books 4 and 9. In Book 4, reason is practical reason only - judgment of the best course to follow in each situation - not the love of wisdom for its own sake that characterizes the philosopher. In the course of distinguishing the parts of the soul, the question arises whether spirit is a distinct element at all, since it seems in some ways to resemble the appetites and in others to resemble reason. The example of Leontius successfully distinguishes spirit from appetite; but the examples chosen to distinguish it from reason are far less telling. Glaucon points out that children lack reason but are full of spirit, and that some adults remain children, in this sense, most of their lives. Socrates adds that the same is true of animals (441b-c). But neither of these examples involves a conflict between spirit and reason. And that is the tool Socrates is using to prise apart the different elements in the soul.

What is more, the example of conflict that Socrates then brings up, of Odysseus reproving his angry heart, is not a fundamental conflict. It is not a conflict such as takes place within Leontius, whose spirit or self-respect recoils at the very same prospect - looking at the ugly or horrific - to which he also feels a fascinated, greedy attraction. Odysseus' reason is in league with his spirit; both are working towards his revenge and self-vindication against the suitors. It is only that spirit is impatient, while reason bides its time.

Not until Socrates assigns reason a goal all its own, in its pursuit of wisdom, does a distinction emerge between reason and spirit as motivating forces. In other words, for the motivations of non-philosophers a bipartite psychological analysis would suffice. There are the goals of self-respect and there are material goals, and reason is a mere executive, balancing the two for their mutual benefit, but without goals of its own. Just so, it is only with the advent of philosophers in Callipolis that the military becomes a class distinct from its rulers, who have something better to do with their lives than serve as generals. And as the philosopher-kings work hard to build loyalty in the army so that they can be true 'auxiliaries' or 'helpers', ἐπίκουροι, so reason in the philosopher is at pains to make spirit its 'ally', σύμμαχος (589b).

There is even an equivalent within the individual for the deception that philosopher-kings practise on the soldiers in order to achieve this result. Reason is a farmer managing livestock, and his task with multiform appetite, the lowest element in the soul, is to domesticate its gentle animal components and prevent the 'wild' ones (ἄγρια) from developing (589b). But spirit is compared to a lion, a wild animal. How is farmer Reason to make such a creature his ally? Not by taming it, but by turning its fierceness to good use; by gently persuading it - as Socrates imagines himself 'gently persuading' the man who praises injustice (πείθωμεν... πρᾴως, 589c) - to turn its essentially amoral fierceness against injustice itself.

Spirit has a natural aversion to the ugly; this is what the example of Leontius ('lion-man') demonstrated. Let it be trained, then, to find 'ugly' (αἰσχρός) all those activities that society rightly deems blameworthy and 'shameful' (τὰ αἰσχρὰ νόμιμα, 589c); let it recoil at the thought of that 'most polluted' (μιαρωτάτῳ) of creatures, the many-headed monster, gaining ascendancy over the person's most divine part, reason; or at the thought of itself reduced from magnificent lion to sinister snake or still uglier - indeed, proverbially ugly - monkey (590b). Let it call 'shameful' (αἰσχρά) those actions that make the gentle the slave of the fierce (589d); and let it fail to notice that it itself is counted among the fierce, and is being deceived into working against its own nature.

This is not a matter of self-deception in the individual, however, but of moral education by parents and those in authority over the young (590e). Spirit is 'deceived' only in the sense that the right education will cause it to act against its own unalloyed nature. Its natural fierceness can be redirected and become the basis of a moral sense. So too the guardian herd, if left to itself, would have an interest in reproducing and growing big rather than being bred for the good of the city. But no group in the city, and no element in the soul, can be left to itself; for none exists in isolation.

Turn now to the relation between reason and the appetites. The man who is Callipolis writ small would be one whose reason is put in authority over his bodily desires by some necessity, begins by excluding from the man's life the unmalleable among those desires (as the adults were sent into the fields), but experiences the power of those that remain as a necessity, towards the satisfaction of which it must therefore work. It does not regard the task as anything noble, and gets true satisfaction only when free to exercise its powers for their own sake (as when philosopher-kings are free to engage in philosophy among themselves), not when it is serving the needs of those other desires.

Compare this result with the description of the just and philosophically inclined individual who figures widely in Book 9, where his life is proved to be the best and most pleasant. Reason in this individual is strong enough to exclude at least from his waking life those bodily desires which, if left to develop in him, would prove unmanageable - what Socrates calls the unnecessary and lawless desires (571b-572b, 589b). Those that remain are the 'necessary' (ἀναγκαῖαι) bodily desires - those that reason has no option but to figure out how to satisfy if the individual is to maintain his physical well-being and so be capable of good philosophic work and more generally of living the philosophic life (581e). These desires, for their part, although exerting all the force of necessity upon reason, nevertheless willingly accept reason's direction, as the obedient citizens accepted the philosopher's rule, in return for security and satisfaction (586e). Socrates compares them to domestic animals (589b).

Even the initial necessity imagined to thrust philosophers into office in the city has its equivalent in the individual, in that his reason is imagined to have come from heaven and to have been incarnated and put in authority over his bodily desires by unavoidable destiny. This is a theme more elaborately treated in dialogues other than the *Republic*, most notably in the *Timaeus* (42a, 69c-d). But it does make its appearance in the *Republic*. It does so first when Socrates claims that whereas other virtues are things of the body, not pre-existing but brought about by habit and practice, the virtue of reason or wisdom is of more divine and permanent stuff (518e). And it does so most importantly in the preamble to the myth of Er, where it is suggested that the soul in its truest form may consist of reason alone, and is crippled by its contact with the body (611c-612a), as well as in the myth itself, where the reincarnation of souls is announced in a decree of Lachesis, who is the daughter of Necessity (617d-e). Those souls may be free to choose their lives, but they are not free to avoid reincarnation.

The difference between levels of the analogy brings with it a difference between the necessity that confronts reason in the philosophic individual and that which confronts the philosopher-king in Callipolis. Socrates and the interlocutors, imagining themselves as founders of the city, impose on the rulers the necessity of caring for the needs of the general citizenry, an imposition that corresponds to the force exerted on reason by the necessary bodily desires. In the individual this force is imposed 'by nature' (τῇ φύσει, 558e) - by the simple presence of inborn and inescapable desires. In the city the corresponding necessity is imposed 'by law' (νόμῳ, 519e) and requires the agency of a go-between, the founders, to make itself felt. It becomes an obligation, albeit one grounded in reasons that the philosopher-king can accept. This is as close an analogy as the city can provide for the power exerted by necessary desires in the virtuous individual.

Certainly, Callipolis is distinct from other cities in being a 'city established on natural principles' (κατὰ φύσιν οἰκισθεῖσα πόλις, 428e); but this does not affect the contrast between necessity imposed by nature and necessity imposed by law. It is significant that the phrase just quoted comes up in the account of the city's wisdom, when we are told that the city is wise by virtue of the understanding possessed by its ruling class. The constitution of Callipolis is in accordance with nature because those who have authority over it are naturally superior individuals (compare 485a). This does not make that constitution any less a creature of convention.

Working out the analogy shows us where the stronger necessity lies, in the individual; yet insisting on the analogy helps us maintain the proper philosophic distance even from that stronger necessity - from the politics of the soul as well as from the politics of the city. The philosopher understands that nature's due ends at the borders of his soul, his inner polity. Society's due has only a derivative force, the necessity of a social obligation, accepted by the philosopher only because he already recognizes nature's due. This attitude may seem to have something in common with that of the 'real man', the 'natural man' of Glaucon's speech in Book 2; for he too believes that nature's due ends at the borders of his soul. His reaction, however, is to think himself entitled thereby to trample society's due as so much convention, to trample it underfoot as if he were a god. The philosopher's recognition of nature's due is the recognition that he is only human, and this readies him to accept his social obligations. He too would rather be a god - although his god is contemplative, not all-powerful. But because he can see himself as a whole, see what is human in him as well as what is godlike, he will agree to look after society as a whole if given the opportunity. He can see little and see big, as no others can; this qualifies him to rule those others. And he will agree to do what he is qualified above all others to do. Why? Because he can see little and see big.

Sources and Scholarly Contexts for Chapter 4

That the metaphors deriving from the city-soul analogy are applied in an asymmetrical fashion does not escape Norbert Blössner's sharp eye. He uses this observation, however, as an argument to support his claim that the tripartition of the soul is determined not by facts of human nature but wholly by context: that is, by the comparison with the three classes in Callipolis and by the intentions of the larger argument in which this comparison has its place (Blössner 1997, pp. 174-78). Taken in itself, Blössner's explanation of the asymmetry is not implausible. To contest it, one would need not only to give an alternative point to the asymmetry, as I have done in this chapter, but also to consider how the tripartite soul is treated in other dialogues, which is beyond the scope of this book.

I have given the asymmetry an alternative point by connecting it with the fact that justice amounts to something more in a man than in a city, despite being analogous in both. That the city is capable of less than the man is something I believe I have learnt from the writings of Leo Strauss and of others influenced by Strauss. See the references in 'Sources and scholarly contexts for chapter 1'. Robert Spaemann also gives a fine treatment of this topic in chapter 8 of Höffe ed., 1997 (esp. p. 170). See also Ferrari ed., 2000, pp. xxv-xxviii.

My discussion of Callipolis as a city in the sky and of its paradigmatic beauty as an artefact of Plato's imagination raises the topic of the *Republic*'s utopianism. The approach taken here belongs to none of the three types that are prominent, although it partakes of each. Call these types the idealistic, the realistic, and the ironic. The first sees Callipolis as an ideal intended primarily to motivate personal morality, and the *Republic* as primarily a moral rather than a political work. Guthrie 1975 and Isnardi Parente 1985 are representative of this approach. The realistic interpretation regards Callipolis as a place that Plato would have wanted to see built, or that he intended at the very least as a blueprint for actual political reform. This approach is particularly well defended in Burnyeat 1992. On the ironic interpretation Callipolis is not just unpracticable, it is not even desirable; yet it *is* a utopia. And what this shows is that conflict between the common good and the good of the individual is ultimate and insoluble. The approach derives from Strauss 1964.

The approach I take in this chapter may be dubbed idealist to the extent that it has Plato regard the imaginary Callipolis, Callipolis-in-the-book, as the most beautiful created city - more beautiful than the built embodiment could be; it may be dubbed realist to the extent that it has Plato regard the built embodiment, nevertheless, as the greater achievement; and to the extent that it emphasizes the philosopher's reserve not only towards the politics of the city but also towards that of the soul, and therefore towards the politics of even the best city, a politics permeated by the best souls, we may call it ironic. Like the ironic approach, it too plays up the theme of compulsion, in its attempt to sound the depths of the philosopher's acceptance of necessity. It does not reduce the philosopher's political 'reluctance' to the level of a response to mundane administrative work and its vexations, in the manner of Kraut 1999. If I had to give my approach a name I would dub it the writerly type, because its most distinctive feature is to see the *Republic* as a political and sincerely utopian work and at the same time as a project of utopian writing, primarily, rather than of utopian reform. Plato set out to do the most beautiful political thing, not the grandest.

In tracing the emergence in the *Republic* of a distinction between reason and spirit as motivating forces I offer a way to resolve a dispute that continues between two parties in the study of the tripartite soul: between those who believe that a bipartite rather than tripartite soul - one divided between reason and desire in a relatively conventional fashion - is fundamental to Plato's psychology, and that 'spirit' is introduced as an intermediate part primarily for the sake of the political analogy; and those on the other hand who take spirit to be a fundamental force in the soul that must be kept distinct from the other fundamental forces. Penner 1971 is an important representative of the first camp, which includes Robinson 1995, pp. 44-46. Norbert Blössner's view, explained at the outset of this section, draws support from this camp but goes well beyond it in arguing that the Platonic dialogues do not propose a Platonic psychology. Price 1995, pp. 68-70, is characteristically subtle and therefore hard to place. He finds the argument for distinguishing the spirited part problematic, not however because a bipartite analysis would be satisfactory, but because even the tripartite analysis is impoverished. The opposite camp, that takes spirit to be a fundamental force, is well represented by Cooper 1984, Reeve 1988, pp. 135-40, and Vegetti ed., 1998 [vol. 3], pp. 29-40. The motivations of the spirited part are of great concern also to writers influenced by Strauss, and it is from Craig 1994 that I take the idea that spirit can be said to have a natural aversion to the ugly.

I agree with the second camp that spirit is a fundamental force in the soul, and is self-assertive in a way that the desires of the appetitive part are not. Anger is characteristic of spirit but is not of its essence, so that the equivalence in some respects of anger and emotions such as grief, which in Book 10 is located in the appetitive part, does not render the spirited part less distinct (*pace* Penner 1971, p. 112). Nevertheless, the first camp are correct when they point out the inadequacies of the argument for tripartition in Book 4 and how in Book 10 a bipartite division suffices. What this indicates, however, is not that the spirited part lacks fundamental status, but that the reasoning part in the souls of non-philosophers is not accorded the fundamental status it merits. In each of us these three elements exist and are fundamental; but except in the souls of philosophers, the reasoning part does not work towards its natural end, but is enslaved to the goals of the other parts. Compare the account of the psychology of the *Protagoras* and *Phaedo* in Ferrari 1990.

References

Andersson 1971: T.J. Andersson, *Polis and Psyche: A Motif in Plato's Republic.* Stockholm, 1971.

Annas 1981: J. Annas, *An Introduction to Plato's Republic.* Oxford, 1981.

Annas 1999: J. Annas, *Platonic Ethics, Old and New.* Ithaca, 1999.

Benardete 1989: S. Benardete, *Socrates' Second Sailing: On Plato's Republic.* Chicago, 1989.

Bloom 1968: A. Bloom trans., *The Republic of Plato* [with interpretive essay]. New York, 1968.

Blössner 1997: N. Blössner, *Dialogform und Argument: Studien zu Platons 'Politeia'.* Stuttgart, 1997.

Brann 1989-90: E. Brann, 'The music of the *Republic*', *The St. John's Review,* double issue 39.1-2 (1989-90) 1-103.

Burnyeat 1992: M.F. Burnyeat, 'Utopianism and fantasy: the practicability of Plato's ideally just city': 175-87 in J. Hopkins and A. Savile eds., *Psychoanalysis, Mind and Art.* Oxford, 1992. [Repr. in Fine 1999]

Burnyeat 2001: M.F. Burnyeat, 'Plato' [a 'Master-Mind' lecture available online 2001 at www.ex.ac.uk/plato/Burnyeat.htm, and forthcoming in the *Proceedings of the British Academy*].

Cambiano 1982: G. Cambiano, 'Patologia e metafora politica. Alcmeone, Platone, *Corpus Hippocraticum*', *Elenchos* 3 (1982) 219-36.

Carter 1986: L. B. Carter, *The Quiet Athenian.* Oxford, 1986.

Cooper 1984: J. Cooper, 'Plato's theory of human motivation', *History of Philosophy Quarterly* 1.1 (1984) 3-21.

Craig 1994: L. Craig, *The War-Lover: A Study of Plato's Republic.* Toronto, 1994.

Donlan 1980: W. Donlan, *The Aristocratic Ideal in Ancient Greece.* Lawrence, 1980.

Dover, 1974: K. J. Dover, *Greek Popular Morality.* Oxford, 1974.

Ferrari 1990: G. R. F. Ferrari, 'Akrasia as neurosis in Plato's *Protagoras*': 115-39 in J.J. Cleary and D. Shartin eds., *Proceedings of the Boston Area Colloquium in Ancient Philosophy,* vol. 6. Lanham, 1990.

Ferrari 1997: G. R. F. Ferrari, 'Strauss' Plato', *Arion* 5.2 (1997) 36-65.

Ferrari ed., 2000: *Plato: The Republic.* Trans. Tom Griffith, ed. (with introduction and notes) G. R. F. Ferrari. [Cambridge Texts in the History of Political Thought.] Cambridge, 2000.

Fine ed., 1999: G. Fine ed., *Plato 2: Ethics, Politics, Religion, and the Soul.* [Oxford Readings in Philosophy.] Oxford, 1999.

Frede 1997: D. Frede, 'Die ungerechte Verfassungen und die ihnen entsprechenden Menschen (Buch VIII 543a-IX 576b)': 251-70 in Höffe ed., 1997.

Gigon 1976: O. Gigon, *Gegenwärtigkeit und Utopie: Eine Interpretation von Platons 'Staat'.* Zürich, 1976.

Gill 1996: C. Gill, *Personality in Greek Epic, Tragedy, and Philosophy: The Self in Dialogue.* Oxford, 1996.

Grote 1885: G. Grote, *Plato and the Other Companions of Sokrates.* 4 vols. London, 1885.

Guthrie 1975: W.K.C. Guthrie, *A History of Greek Philosophy,* vol. 4 [Plato: the man and his dialogues, earlier period]. Cambridge, 1975.

Hobbs 2000: A. Hobbs, *Plato and the Hero.* Cambridge, 2000.

Höffe ed., 1997: O. Höffe ed., *Platon: Politeia.* Berlin, 1997.

Howland 1993: J. Howland, *The Republic: The Odyssey of Philosophy.* [Twayne's Masterwork Studies.] Toronto, 1993.

Irwin 1995: T. Irwin, *Plato's Ethics.* Oxford, 1995.

Isnardi Parente 1985: M. Isnardi Parente, 'Motivi utopistici - ma non utopia - in Platone': 137-54 in Renato Uglione ed., *La Città Ideale nella Tradizione Classica e Biblico-Cristiana.* Torino, 1985.

Johnstone 1994: S. Johnstone, 'Virtuous toil, vicious work: Xenophon on aristocratic style', *Classical Philology* 89.3 (1994) 219-40.

Kahn 1987: C. Kahn, 'Plato's theory of desire', *Review of Metaphysics* 41 (1987) 77-103.

Kraut 1999: R. Kraut, 'Return to the Cave: *Republic* 519-521': 235-54 in Fine ed., 1999.

Lear 1992: J. Lear, 'Inside and outside the *Republic*', *Phronesis* 37.2 (1992) 184-215. [Reprinted with minor alterations of format in his *Open Minded: Working Out the Logic of the Soul.* Cambridge, Mass., 1998.]

Penner 1971: T. Penner, 'Thought and desire in Plato': 96-118 in G. Vlastos ed., *Plato: A Collection of Critical Essays,* vol. 2. Notre Dame, 1971.

Price 1995: A.W. Price, *Mental Conflict.* [Issues in Ancient Philosophy.] London, 1995.

Reeve 1988: C.D.C. Reeve, *Philosopher-Kings: The Argument of Plato's Republic.* Princeton, 1988.

Robinson 1995: T.M. Robinson, *Plato's Psychology.* 2nd ed., Toronto, 1995.

Strauss 1964: L. Strauss, *The City and Man.* Chicago, 1964.

Sullivan 1997: S. D. Sullivan, *Aeschylus' Use of Psychological Terminology.* Montreal, 1997.

Sullivan 1999: S. D. Sullivan, *Sophocles' Use of Psychological Terminology.* Carleton University Press, 1999.

Sullivan 2000: S. D. Sullivan, *Euripides' Use of Psychological Terminology.* Montreal, 2000.

Vegetti 1983: M. Vegetti, *Tra Edipo e Euclide.* Milano, 1983.

Vegetti ed., 1998: *Platone: La Repubblica.* Traduzione e commento a cura di M. Vegetti. Napoli, 1998.

White 1984: N. White, 'The classification of goods in Plato's *Republic*', *Journal of the History of Philosophy* 22 (1984) 393-421.

Whitehead 1977: D. Whitehead, *The Ideology of the Athenian Metic.* Cambridge Philological Society suppl. vol. 4, 1977.

Williams 1973: B. Williams, 'The analogy of city and soul in Plato's *Republic*': 196-206 in E.N. Lee et al. eds., *Exegesis and Argument (Phronesis* suppl. vol. 1) 1973. [Repr. in Fine 1999.]

Index Locorum

Aeschylus
Agamemnon
1106: 63
Choephoroe
934: 63
Persae
169: 63
767: 62

Alcmeon
fr. B4, Diels-Kranz: 64

[Anonymous]
On Tropes (*Rhet. Graec.*,
Spengel, vol. 3, p. 228): 85

Aristophanes
Acharnians
480-4: 62
Knights
1417: 63
Peace
642: 63

Aristotle
Nicomachean Ethics
1097a15-b6: 17
1124b9-10: 24
1124b17-23: 24
Poetics
21, 1457b: 61n
Politics
4.9.3, 1294a39-95b1: 104
Rhetoric
3.4.4, 1407a: 61
3.10.7, 1411a: 61

'Demetrius'
On Style
78: 61, 85

Democritus
fr. B236, Diels-Kranz: 62
fr. B290, Diels-Kranz: 63

Euripides
fr. 136, Nauck: 65
fr. 718.1: 62
Hippolytus
538: 65
Medea
1021-80: 62

Gorgias
Helen
8: 62

Heraclitus
fr. B85, Diels-Kranz: 62

Isocrates
Areopagiticus
14: 103, 104
Letter to the Sons of Jason
11-12: 88
Panathenaicus
138: 103
To Demonicus
21: 88
To Nicocles
5: 88
6: 88
29: 88
31: 89

592b: 104, 107
Book 10
608c: 32
608d: 33
611c: 31
611c-612a: 31, 114
612a: 32
613c: 32
614a: 32
617d-e: 114
617e: 107
618b, d: 18
621d: 32
Seventh Letter
324c-326b: 11
327e: 108
328c-d: 109
341c: 110
344b: 110
Symposium
208c-d: 21
Timaeus
34b: 106
41a-d: 106
42a: 114
47b: 105, 106
47c: 104
69c-d: 114

Sophocles
Trachiniae
441-44: 65

Stobaeus
Diels-Kranz 1.64.10: 87

Theognis
39, West: 63
630-1: 62

Thucydides
2.40.2: 22
8.68.1: 26

Xenophon
Anabasis
1.9.1: 103
Cyropaedia
1.6.8: 87
Memorabilia
3.2.2: 87
3.6: 13
Symposium
3.5: 12